THE CONSORTIUM

A Journal of Classical Christian Education

THE CONSORTIUM

A Journal of Classical Christian Education

Promoting classical education and fostering human flourishing for generations to come.

Volume 2, Issue 1

The Consortium: A Journal of Classical Christian Education
Volume 2, Issue 1.

Copyright © 2023 by Roman Roads Press

Published by Roman Roads Press in collaboration with Kepler Education and The Consortium of Classical Educators

Moscow, Idaho
info@romanroadspress.com | romanroadspress.com

Editorial Advisory Board:

- Dr. Scott Postma, Editor in Chief
- Dr. Robert M. Woods, Senior Contributing Editor
- Dr. Gregory Soderberg, Contributing Editor

Interior Layout by Carissa Hale

All rights reserved. No part of this publication may be reproduced, stored in a retrieval system, or transmitted in any form by any means, electronic, mechanical, photocopy, recording, or otherwise, without prior permission of the publisher, except as provided by the USA copyright law.

Licensing and permissions: info@romanroadspress.com

ISBN: 978-1-944482-81-7

Version 1.0.0   June 2023

Contents

Introduction
by Scott Postma, PhD   1

Where Has All the Beauty Gone?
by Michael R. Young, PhD   15

The Beautiful Art of Brokenness:
A Review of *Rembrandt is in the Wind* by Russ Ramsey
by Sarah Abbott, MA   33

Vast Beauty and Staggering Wonder:
Putting the Childlike Spirit Back into Education
by Junius Johnson, PhD   39

Review of *Mr. Bliss* by J. R. R. Tolkien
by Christy Anne Vaughan, EdD   51

The Aesthetics of Humility
by Gregory Soderberg, PhD   55

Review of *In the Beauty of Holiness: Art and the Bible in Western Culture* by David Lyle Jeffrey
by Robert M. Woods, PhD   83

The Question of the Nude:
Guidance for Classical Christian Educators

by Joshua Herring, MDiv   89

Wonder and Monsters

by James C. McGlothlin, PhD   113

THE CONSORTIUM

A Journal of Classical Christian Education

INTRODUCTION

by Scott Postma, PhD

At the heart of the movement for the renewal of classical Christian education is the recovery not only of truth and goodness, but also of beauty and wonder. Beauty has long been considered by many to be part of the triad of transcendentals, joining itself with goodness and truth. Wonder, on the other hand, is not transcendental, per se, but lends to the pursuit of goodness, truth, and beauty. Wonder can be defined as "a person, thing, or event that excites surprise; a strange thing; a cause of astonishment or admiration; a prodigy, a miracle. 2. the feeling of surprise, admiration, and awe which is caused by something new, unusual, strange, great, extraordinary, or not well understood."[1] While it is also more than this, wonder is largely the engine that drives our pursuits of goodness, truth, and beauty. As a matter of fact, wonder is the beginning of all philosophy according to Socrates who says, "This sense of wonder is the mark of the philosopher. Philosophy indeed has no other origin" (*Theatetus* 155d). For Socrates, wonder is akin to Eros, the "primitive intellectual impulse" that compels a man to pursue a woman, a philoso-

---

1 Webster's Dictionary, *Webster's Dictionary: New Twentieth Century* (Cleveland, OH: World, 1962), 2103.

pher to seek knowledge, and a child to ask, "Why is the sky blue?" In the *Symposium*, Diotima tells Socrates,

> Whoever has been initiated so far in the mysteries of love and has viewed all these aspects of the beautiful in due succession, is at last drawing near the final revelation. And now, Socrates, there bursts upon him that wondrous vision which is the very soul of beauty he has toiled so long for. (*Symposium*, 210e)

Socrates learns from Diotima that Eros is like a ladder which leads the beholder upward from the wonder of and desire for the corporeal "body" to the wonder of and desire for intellectual contemplation of the Forms (the ultimate reality). Wonder, then, is a compelling love for that which delights us but is not fully comprehended, a desire borne up of love which carries us toward a fuller knowledge and experience of beauty, truth, and goodness.

Speaking of what delights us, Thomas Aquinas notably defined beauty as *"id quod visum placet,"* that which is pleasing upon being seen. On its face, this definition of beauty is straightforward and satisfying. But, upon further consideration, maybe it is not such a complete definition after all. For instance, can it not be said that some music is beautiful? Beautiful music is something pleasing to the ear, not something pleasing to see. And, if we grant that Aquinas simply meant "seen" as synecdoche for the sensual (all five senses), what about the location of beauty? Does it exist in the object observed (art) or heard (music) or experienced (nature), or does beauty reside in the subject experiencing the art (i.e., the eye of the beholder)? Also, is beauty actually a universal concept, a transcendent idea like goodness and truth? For example, what if the thing seen, or heard, or experienced is

Introduction

not pleasing to all people? Finally, how do we actually experience beauty? Do we *actually* experience it in the senses or the intellect?

Questions about the definition of beauty abound, making it a bit more difficult to pin down. Thus, if beauty were simple to define, there would be little to discuss. But as Tolstoy recognized, "The notion of art as the manifestation of beauty is not at all as simple as it seems, especially now when our senses of touch, taste, and smell are included in it, as they are by the latest aestheticians."[2] Therefore, in the philosophy of modern aesthetics, the controversy is in determining if there is such a thing as beauty, and if there is, how exactly should it be defined?

To answer these questions and establish a conceptual definition of beauty many have turned to analyzing our transcendent triad: truth, goodness, and beauty. Truth is the objective of knowledge, particularly that which relates to properly functioning human reason and empirical evidence. It is possible to strive for objectivity in truth by distinguishing between objective facts—for which sound argumentation and appeals to evidence can help facilitate agreement—and subjective taste for which minimal agreement should be expected. For example, some people prefer the color red to the color green. That is okay. However, all drivers in the U.S. ought to stop when the traffic light is red and go when the traffic light is green. Goodness, in similar fashion, is the objective of the will, particularly as it relates to human satisfaction. Happiness, being the chief good in classical thought, is that for which all other goods are desired. One can strive to-

---

[2] Leo Tolstoy, *What is Art?*, trans. Richard Pevear and Larissa Volokhonsky (New York: Penguin Books, 1995), 12.

ward objectivity in goodness by distinguishing between what Mortimer Adler calls real and apparent goods. He explains,

> Real goods...are relative not to individual desires, but to desires inherent in human nature and so are the same for all human beings. To the extent that human nature is everywhere and at all times the same (this is, as long as the species persists in its specific characteristics), real goods have the universality and immutability that gives them objectivity...Apparent goods are relative to individual desires and are, therefore, subjective.[3]

Because of the relationship of goodness to truth, some human desires—those based on taste and not truth—are subjective, not prescriptive. One person's taste for seafood is not something that ought to be desired by everyone. Some people prefer steak. As the saying goes, *De gustibus non disputandum est*.[4] Nevertheless, all humans ought to desire a diet that promotes health and satisfaction. The need and desire to eat nutritious food is universal to all humans, therefore it is a good. But it is not an ultimate good. The highest good is happiness.[5] The highest good is an end in itself, and it is for this good all other goods are sought.

Beauty, however, while related to goodness and truth, is a bit of a different thing. It is, in fact, a kind of goodness in that it is something to be desired. Also, it is related to truth in that it is something to be known. Yet beauty is still

---

3   Mortimer J. Adler, *Six Great Ideas* (New York: Simon & Schuster, 1997), 100.

4   Translated, "there is no debating about tastes."

5   Depending on which philosopher or authority one consults, happiness is understood as *eudaimonia* (when one's soul is well-ordered toward human flourishing: *eu*=good/*daimon*=spirit) or God (Whom, in Christian orthodoxy, is to be glorified and enjoyed forever).

Introduction

elusive. Even the conservative philosopher and critic, Roger Scruton, insightfully acknowledges, "The status of beauty as an ultimate value is questionable, in the way that the status of truth and goodness are not."[6] In a day where relativism and extreme skepticism seems to rule, one can plausibly argue an objective orientation for truth and goodness, but arguing an objective center for beauty is not nearly as easy. Nevertheless, Scruton contends that even though you may not be able to explain why exactly, "You want the table, the room or the website to look right, and looking right matters in the way that beauty generally matters—not by pleasing the eye only, but by conveying meanings and values which have weight for you and which you are consciously putting on display."[7] Although it is difficult to establish its boundaries and characteristics, there is something intangible about beauty, something transcendent that one cannot put his finger on. Beauty is something everyone recognizes when it is there, but no one knows exactly how to describe it. Mortimer J. Adler notes this as well, saying, "There is less that can be said about beauty with clarity and precision than can be said about truth and goodness."[8] In any case, challenging as it may be, it does not preclude a thorough treatment of what *can* be known and what *cannot* be known about this transcendent concept.

I previously quoted from Thomas Aquinas, who was one of the first to treat the idea of beauty in the context of an aesthetic philosophy (before this category of inquiry was given the name "aesthetics"). In his *Summa Theologica*, he posited,

---

[6] Roger Scruton, *Beauty: A Very Short Introduction* (Oxford: Oxford University Press, 2011), 3.

[7] Scruton, *Beauty*, 8.

[8] Adler, *Six Great Ideas*, 104.

> beauty relates to the cognitive faculty; for beautiful things are those which please when seen. Hence beauty consists in due proportion; for the senses delight in things duly proportioned, as in what is after their own kind—because even sense is a sort of reason, just as is every cognitive faculty. Now, since knowledge is by assimilation, and similarity relates to form, beauty properly belongs to the nature of a formal cause.[9]

In its most fundamental essence, Aquinas relates beauty to the sense of sight and to the cognitive faculties. He even posits that the senses—seeing, hearing, touching, smelling, tasting—are themselves a sort of cognitive faculty. Later, during the Enlightenment period, a distinction was made between the senses and the cognition, but for our purposes, it is noteworthy that Aquinas relates one's ability to see form and proportion in an object and reason whether such is pleasing or not. It further appears that Aquinas assumes some measure of the universal subjectivity in what will later become Kant's aesthetic formulation. Aquinas continues his treatment of the beautiful as a concept that is related to goodness:

> The beautiful is the same as the good, and they differ in aspect only. For since good is what all seek, the notion of good is that which calms the desire; while the notion of the beautiful is that which calms the desire, by being seen or known. Consequently those senses chiefly regard the beautiful, which are the most cognitive, viz., sight and hearing, as ministering to reason; for we speak of beautiful

---

9 Saint Thomas Aquinas, *The Summa Theologica*, ed. Mortimer J. Adler, Philip W. Goetz, and Daniel J. Sullivan, trans. Laurence Shapcote, Second Edition., vol. 17, Great Books of the Western World (Chicago; Auckland; Geneva; London; Madrid; Manila; Paris; Rome; Seoul; Sydney; Tokyo; Toronto: Robert P. Gwinn; Encyclopædia Britannica, Inc., 1990), 26.

sights and beautiful sounds. But in reference to the other objects of the other senses, we do not use the expression *beautiful*, for we do not speak of beautiful tastes, and beautiful odours. Thus it is evident that beauty adds to goodness a relation to the cognitive faculty: so that *good* means that which simply pleases the appetite; while the *beautiful* is something pleasant to apprehend.[10]

In Aquinas's expanded definition, the beautiful is related to "being seen or known," in the same way goodness is related to "desire." They are, in essence, the same thing, but differ only in one aspect. In the same way all seek the good (whether real or apparent) to satisfy a desire, all seek the beautiful to satisfy a desire. What is different is the means of satisfaction. Satisfaction, or pleasure, is something all people seek naturally. When it is cold, human beings seek the good of shelter or clothing. When someone is hungry or thirsty, he seeks the good of food and drink. There are other pleasures people seek as well, like wealth, health, knowledge, and friendship. When people obtain or possess those things which calm the desire, they are pleased or satisfied. As previously mentioned, the only difference between goodness and beauty for Aquinas is the means of satisfaction. He explains that the desire for the beautiful is calmed by that which can be seen or known. In essence, the good is something pleasant to the appetite, whether real or perceived; the beautiful is something pleasant to apprehend, whether by seeing it or contemplating it.

Aquinas further provides qualifications to his definition of the beautiful. In other words, not everything is beautiful just because it might seem pleasant to look at or apprehend. He explains, "For beauty includes three conditions, *integrity*

---

10   Aquinas, *The Summa Theologica*, 737.

or *perfection*, since those things which are impaired are by the very fact ugly; due *proportion* or *harmony*; and lastly, *brightness*, or *clarity*, whence things are called beautiful which have a bright color."[11] It is noted that Aquinas presupposes ugliness to establish qualifications for his definition of beauty, but it should also be noted that his treatment of beauty is not an aesthetic treatment in the way aesthetics have been treated since the Renaissance or the Enlightenment.

Aquinas is deriving his definitions effectual of his treatment of the good. Recall, goodness is the objective of the will, particularly as it relates to human satisfaction. The good is what humans universally desire because it is inherent in human nature to desire such. To have two legs, for example, is what all rational human beings desire. It is true that there are some, small in number, who find pleasure in pain or have some sort of body dysmorphic disorder, and thus find pleasure in mutilation. These are abnormal circumstances, and anomalies and mental-illness should not define what is normal. Aside from such abnormality, no one desires only one leg—or a malformed face, or an extra appendage. Any of these would be considered *malus* (i.e., bad). Granting that there are degrees of goodness and degrees of badness, speaking rationally of the human species, one can confidently say, one leg is bad; two legs are good. It is in this context that Aquinas discusses beauty.

On the other hand, there is a sense in which beauty is subjective if we distinguish between enjoyable beauty and admirable beauty, but what Aquinas has in mind is what Adler calls admirable beauty. Admiral beauty is related to truth whereas enjoyable beauty is related to taste. One person pre-

---

11 Aquinas, *The Summa Theologica*, 211.

fers red wine to white wine, and another prefers whiskey to beer. These are matters of taste in the realm of goodness. One person prefers the Van Goghs to the Cezannes, and another person prefers landscapes to human forms. This is enjoyable beauty. Admirable beauty, however, is concerned with the integrity of the painting, or the poem, or the architecture. Integrity refers to the inner consistency of a thing, as well as its possessing and displaying all of the requisite parts consistent with the nature of its being. Admirable beauty is also concerned with the harmony or the proportions of an object.

Proportion is an object's intrinsic approximation to itself, or the "correspondence between inner and outer reality, appearance and essence, matter and form."[12] Finally, admirable beauty is concerned with the radiance of an object, its brightness or clarity. In a sense, it is related to the Greek idea of δοξα, meaning splendor or glory.[13] Again, it is in the context of admiral beauty and not enjoyable beauty that Aquinas provides this definition. On this particular conceptualization of beauty, Scruton rightly observes, "According to this idea beauty is an ultimate value—something that we pursue for its own sake, and for the pursuit of which no further reason need be given."[14]

On the foundation of what has been said, I would argue there is a viable conceptual basis for beauty that is rooted in truth and goodness: simply put, true beauty is in the qualities that give rise to our delight. It is an admirable beauty in the objective sense (it rests in the object itself). Additionally, as

---

12 Robert E. Wood, *Placing Aesthetics: Reflections on the Philosophic Tradition (Series in Continental thought; 26)* (Athens, OH: Ohio University Press, 1999), 109.

13 Wood, *Placing Aesthetics*, 105.

14 Scruton, *Beauty*, 2.

an ultimate good, it is desirable of our rational senses (cognition acting on that which is perceived by the senses) the same way truth is desirable of reason and happiness is desirable of the will. To desire ugliness would be as unnatural as desiring unhappiness or fallacy. On the other hand, enjoyable beauty, as it has thus been designated, is simply a matter of taste. It is subjective (it rests in the observer, listener, etc.). There is no point in arguing about matters of preference where the admirable qualities of beauty are not in question. As with goodness, so with enjoyable beauty. Recall, *De gustibus non disputandum est.* Where the admirable qualities are in question, reason and empirical facts can be used in rational dialogue among those with superior faculties of judgment to achieve some degree of consensus. This, of course, brings up a new set of questions: is that not an aristocratic (bourgeois) concept? And, does it not fly in the face of our democratic sentiments? In other words, if there are superior judges, who decides they are superior? What is the standard for that?

I will not answer those questions here as I have already addressed them in the first issue of volume one of *The Consortium*. Instead, I present to you a host of essays and book reviews that attempt in various ways to make progress toward providing a fuller understanding of the concepts of wonder and beauty. In Michael Young's essay, "Where Has All the Beauty Gone?," he addresses Maxwell L. Anderson's concern that "over the last thirty years in his travels to visit with artists from around the world he had not heard any artist bring up the subject of beauty in relation to their work." Anderson is the former Director of the Dallas Museum of Art, whose ethos in the art world should cause us to ask, "How could this be? Why would there be an absence of beauty from artists' works and vision for their projects?" Young addresses the

Introduction

many possibilities of the culture's neglect of beauty, including beauty's elusive definition. Young ponders the questions, opining that,

> One can only conjecture; an emphasis on social justice, a consuming vision of a dystopian world, various philosophies that undermine meaning and truth, sensitive souls overwrought over the suffering visible in the world? Regardless of the many streams of thought and reactions that might contribute to such a neglect or denial of beauty in artistic endeavors, it does stir one to wonder, where has all the beauty gone, long time passing?

In "The Beautiful Art of Brokenness," Sarah Abbott reviews Russ Ramsey's book, *Rembrandt is in the Wind*, in which he contends that our brokenness can reveal transcendent beauty. Abbott claims that "by transporting us into the lives of nine different artists, Ramsey offers his readers 'a rich portrayal of beauty…[that] teaches us to appreciate the genuine value of brokenness, and leaves us pondering deeply challenging questions of these real people who, in many ways, mirror our own lives.'"

And, in "Vast Beauty and Staggering Wonder: Putting the Childlike Spirit Back into Education," Junius Johnson argues that the recovery of wonder is paramount to the recovery of a proper philosophy of education and to do so "we should look to the experts: children." Distinguishing between the modern concept of "child-led learning," Johnson follows the guidance of C. S. Lewis by arguing that "the child*like* experience of learning should be the ground of our educational design. Only we must always remember the important distinction between the child*like* and the child*ish*." In other words, adults are the educators but it is only by awakening the child's loves—his wonder for the things of the world—that the teacher will be able to accomplish "child-leading" (*paedogogia*).

Published posthumously, Tolkien's lesser known children's book, *Mr. Bliss*, is the subject of Christy Vaughan's delightful book review. A splendid manifestation of beauty and wonder, *Mr. Bliss* "overflows with whimsy and silliness in a sweet, bedtime story type of way." Meant to rival Lewis Carroll's *Alice's Adventures in Wonderland*, Vaughan suggests that Tolkien's *Mr. Bliss* "is written as a simple, funny fantasy to be read to small children" as it is "not as dark or violent as Carroll's *Alice's Adventures in Wonderland*."

Next, deriving the framework for his thesis from John Frame's perspectivalism, Gregory Soderberg treats the importance of humility as an operational-principle in the life of an artist in his essay, "The Aesthetics of Humility." Soderberg argues that artists inherently work in relationship to their work, their audience, and their God. And while they may not have time to think through all of the deep, philosophical implications of everything they do in relation to all three aspects of their craft, they can create in a spirit of humility. Soderberg says, "Artists should be primarily humble towards God, towards their audience, and toward their work. The artist must work within norms, within community, within his own aesthetic sense. There is danger of erring in any of these three areas."

Another important work treated in this issue of *The Consortium*, this one reviewed by Robert Woods, is David Lyle Jeffrey's *Beauty of Holiness: Art and the Bible in Western Culture*. Engaging and discussing the "life works of the past two thousand years," Woods suggests Jeffrey's book can be read as "the antidote to the toxic death culture." Woods explains

Introduction

this is a book embodying "more than four decades of reverent scholarship," which "explores the interplay of the Bible and art" "in terms of a story—beginning with the catacombs, rich with imagery, to select modern examples." Simply put, Jeffrey's lovely work explores and evaluates the "trajectory for Christian art in the west."

"The Question of the Nude: Guidance for Classical Christian Educators," by Joshua Herring is a timely piece that investigates the beauty and wonder of the human body in light of modernist's propagation of confusion and the Christian's concerns with holiness. In this paper, Herring addresses the question nearly every parent asks when first encountering nude art in classical art: How should Christian parents, students, and classical educators think about nudity in art?

Finally, James C. McGlothlin closes the issue by seeking to provide a definition and conceptualization of wonder classical educators should seek to evoke within their students. In his essay, he probes the ways in which aesthetic experiences can be a source of such wonder, namely through its connection to beauty. Paradoxically, he goes on to argue that "at least one type of aesthetic experience of ugliness, i.e., good literature that contains monsters, can serve as an avenue for producing this wonder." He grounds his arguments in J. R. R. Tolkien's famous literary defense of monsters within *Beowulf*, showing that literary monsters—and thus some aesthetic experiences of ugliness—can be conducive to classical education's goal to instill wonder within students.

Once again, it is my hope, as well as the hope of our board, that readers will be edified by what is presented in this issue, and through these essays discover the beauty of classical Christian education as well as that unique feature which makes pursuing such an education so wonderful. On behalf of the editorial board and the entire Consortium of Classical Educators, it is by God's Grace and for his Glory that I present to you Volume 2, Summer Issue of *The Consortium: A Journal of Classical Christian Education.*

Dr. Scott Postma
Editor in Chief

Editorial Advisory Board

Dr. Scott Postma—*Editor in Chief*
Dr. Robert M. Woods—*Senior Contributing Editor*
Dr. Gregory Soderberg—*Contributing Editor*

Where Has All the Beauty Gone?[1]

by Michael R. Young, PhD

Introduction

There is much in our current cultural context to provide fodder for thought toward the end of things. Realities such as international terrorism, China and North Korean tensions, the Ukraine and Russian conflict, mass shootings, and a vague sense of national and international order are eroding. The article headline from *USA Today* (9/30/17), captures a pervasive sentiment, "Hurricanes, Earthquakes, Terrorism, Mass Shootings, What's Next?" Apocalyptic visions are played out on television (e.g., *The Walking Dead*, which ended its eleventh season Nov. 20, 2022; thank goodness!) and in movies, too numerous to name. But the present élan to portray order and life ending is certainly not a recent development. One could readily reference the world wars, the holocaust, purges of Stalin and Pol Pot, along with the nuclear standoff of the twentieth century. My attention, however, is toward that which is considered to have already ended or at

---

1   Portions of this article were previously presented at the 2018 *Journal of Faith and the Academy Conference*, and later published in the *Journal of Faith and the Academy*, Vol. XI, No. 2, Fall 2018, under the title, "Beauty Will Save the World"—And Education?

least to be woefully neglected, namely, beauty. By contrast, the subject seems insignificant in the face of the horrors mentioned, but the absence or neglect of beauty and the "cult of the ugly"[2] may well be one of the contributing sources for these cited man made tragedies.

I underscore the increasing loss or attention to beauty by means of comments like this from the speculative theorist and philosopher, G. W. F. Hegel: "Art no longer counts for us as the highest manner in which truth obtains existence for itself...[I]n its highest determination, vocation, and purpose [*Bestimmung*], art is and remains for us...a thing of the past."[3] Further, we have this assertion from within the circles of art practitioners and supporters. The recent past Director of the Dallas Museum of Art, Maxwell L. Anderson, stated in a conference entitled, "Christianity and the Arts," that over the last thirty years in his travels to visit with artists from around the world he had not heard any artist bring up the subject of beauty in relation to their work.[4] How could this be? Why would there be an absence of beauty from artists' works and vision for their projects? One can only conjecture; an emphasis on social justice, a consuming vision of a dystopian

---

2 Michael Martin De Sapio, "The Messiah's Beauty." *Touchstone: A Journal of Mere Christianity*, November/December, 2017, 12. De Sapio is referring to Benedict XVI's expression in the chapter, "Wounded by the Arrow of Beauty: The Cross and the New 'Aesthetics' of Faith," from Benedict's book, *On the Way to Jesus Christ* (San Francisco: Ignatius Press, 2005). For an example of the "cult of the ugly" in practice, see the article, "Windowless Bedrooms Should Never Be an Option. Let's Ban Them for Good." *Texas Architecture* September/October 2022. The author cites University of Texas dormitories built with no windows in the rooms. Such practices were banned in prisons in 1903!

3 G. W. F. Hegel, *Introductory Lectures on Aesthetics*, trans. Bernard Bosanquet (London: Penguin Books, 1993), PLT 80/GA 68. See pages 46–61 for his argument that the purpose of art is the revelation of truth.

4 This is a substantive paraphrase of Director Maxwell's comments at the conference, "Christianity and the Arts." Dallas, Texas, November, 2015.

world, various philosophies that undermine meaning and truth, sensitive souls overwrought over the suffering visible in the world? Regardless of the many streams of thought and reactions that might contribute to such a neglect or denial of beauty in artistic endeavors, it does stir one to wonder, where has all the beauty gone, long time passing?[5]

Perhaps contributing to this neglect of beauty is the mystery of beauty itself, what it is, and how it affects us. Hence, the goal of this paper is to attempt a definition (or at least a description of beauty) and wonder with the latter to serve as a means of recovering the longing for and the creation of the beautiful.

Attempts at Defining Beauty

Let us begin by putting aside the old adage, "beauty is in the eyes of the beholder." Such a claim makes beauty relative to each person's own personal tastes and preferences and thus, beauty is completely subjective and has no objective reality. But here is the objective reality: all people, everywhere, through all of history have acknowledged things as being beautiful. This is fact, so there must be something real about beauty. One certain affirmation of the reality of beauty is our reaction to it. Note one of philosopher Ludwig Wittgenstein's suggestive comments about beauty:

> If I say A has beautiful eyes someone may ask me: what do you find beautiful about his eyes, and perhaps I shall reply:

---

[5] My apologies to Peter, Paul, and Mary for borrowing from their 1962 song, "Where Have All the Flowers Gone?"

the almond shape, long eye-lashes, delicate lids. What do these eyes have in common with a gothic church I find beautiful too? Should I say they make a similar impression on me? What if I were to say that in both cases my hand feels tempted to draw them? That at any rate would be a *narrow definition* of the beautiful.[6]

The impulse to draw the eyes or the church building is the impulse to imitate. This one of the effects beauty has on us, we want to imitate it. Add to this another effect, the desire to share our experience of the beautiful. Elaine Scarry writes:

> This impulse toward a distribution across perceivers is, as both museums and postcards verify, the most common response to beauty: 'Addis is full of blossoms. Wish you were here.' 'The nightingale sang again last night. Come here as soon as you can.'[7]

Then to round out the effects of beauty on us, there is the impulse to express ourselves as we imitate and share our personal encounter with the beautiful. We want to express ourselves in being alive with beauty. Imitation, sharing, self-expression, these three, are universal effects of beauty upon us. But let us press on to seek what beauty might be in and of itself by listening to some of the great minds that have gone before us.

A study of Plato on beauty must begin with a clarification of terminology. The Greek adjective *kalon* only approx-

---

  6   As quoted by Nick Riggle in his online article in Aeon, Dec. 23, 2022, and adapted from his book, *This Beauty: A Philosophy of Being Alive* (New York: Basic Books, 2022).

  7   Elaine Scarry, *On Beauty and Being Just* (Princeton, NJ: Princeton University Press, 2001) as quoted by Riggle in Aeon online magazine, Dec. 23, 2022.

imates the English "beautiful," so that not everything Plato says about a *kalos*, *kalē*, or *kalon* thing refers to his theory of aesthetics. Often the term points to that which is fine, appropriate, noble, admirable or, significantly, to that which is good (*agathon*). This stirs up Plato's thought of his triadic connection between the Good, the Beautiful, and the One or the True (*alethes*). These three form the transcendentals that correspond to mankind's capacity to think (science; truth), to wish (arts; beauty), and to feel (religion; good).[8] Returning to the collection of terms for beauty, the noun *kallos* more readily matches our general use of the term beautiful by referring to beautiful physical objects, but Plato is also cautious about the desire that such physical, visual attractiveness arouses in the soul.

His *Hippias Major* addresses the subject of beauty and, despite the typical form of the dialogues with their inconclusiveness, *Hippias Major* reflects the view of beauty found in other dialogues and perhaps especially in the more familiar *Symposium*. Stanford's Encyclopedia of Philosophy provides a handy three-point summary:

1. Beauty behaves as canonical Platonic Forms do. It possesses the reality that Forms have and is discovered through the same dialectic that brings other Forms to light. Socrates wants Hippias to explain the property that is known when any examples of beauty are known (*essence* of beauty), the *cause* of all occurrences of beauty, and more precisely the cause not of the

---

8 Aristotle is the first to employ the term *transcendental* for the good, beautiful, and true since they transcend (*uperbainein huperbainein*) his ten categories. Aristotle, *Categorie*, trans. E. M. Edghill in *The Basic Works of Aristotle*, ed. Richard McKeon (New York: Random House, 1941), 3–37.

appearance of beauty but of its *real being* (286d, 287c, 289d, 292c, 294e, 297b).

2. Nevertheless, beauty is not just any Form. It bears close relationship to the good (296d), even though Socrates argues that the two are distinct (296e ff., 303e ff.). It is therefore a Form of a status above that of other Forms.

3. Socrates and Hippias appeal to artworks as examples of beautiful things but do not treat those as the central cases (290a–b, 297e–298a). So too generally Plato conducts his inquiry into beauty at a distance from his discussion of art. (There are exceptions to this in the *Republic* and the *Laws*).[9]

These three aspects of Platonic beauty work together and reflect beauty's unique place in Plato's metaphysics, something almost both visible and intelligible.

Philosopher and hermeneutician, H. G. Gadamer, comments on Plato's depiction of the relationship between the beautiful and the good as well as for an initial definition of beautiful; actually, he draws upon Plato, Pythagoras, and Aristotle for his understanding of the beautiful:

> Plato defines the beautiful in terms of measure, appropriateness, and right proportions; and Aristotle states that the elements (eide) of the beautiful are order (taxis), right proportions (summetria), and definition (horismenon), and he finds these paradigmatically exemplified in mathematics. Further, the close connection between the mathematical orders of the beautiful and the order of the heavens means

---

9 Stanford Encyclopedia of Philosophy http://plato.stanford.edu/beauty (accessed Nov. 20).

that the cosmos, the model of all visible harmony, is at the same time the supreme example of beauty in the visible sphere. Harmonious proportion, symmetry, is the decisive condition of all beauty.[10]

This definition manifests the close association between the idea of the beautiful and the teleological order of being as based on Pythagoras's and Plato's concepts of measure, as well as indicating the beautiful's universal ontology. Gadamer continues his reference to Plato, finding further hermeneutical insight from the very nature of the beautiful.

Though the idea of the beautiful is closely linked in Plato with the idea of the good, Gadamer does point out that Plato distinguishes the two concepts, with special advantage reserved for the beautiful. While both the good and the beautiful manifest a harmony between the thing and its disclosure, the good cannot be fully grasped for it takes flight into the beautiful. The beautiful can be grasped due to its visible manifestations while the good is not always clearly visible. As an example, the good of human virtue is only obscurely discerned from the unclear medium of appearances, but the beautiful has its own radiance favorably disposing people toward it. Gadamer cites Plato's statement, "Beauty alone has this quality: that it is what is most radiant (ekphanestaton) and lovely."[11]

With Plato's aesthetics serving as a bit of an anchor for our investigation, what follows is a running list of attempts to define the beautiful. It is not a thorough list, nor does it provide thorough explications of each entry's definition. Rather,

---

10 H. G. Gadamer, *Truth and Method*, 479; *WM* 454.

11 Gadamer, *Truth and Method*, 481; *WM*, 456. The citation is from *Phraedrus*, 250d 7.

it is to display some of the range of definitions or descriptions of art and beauty, simultaneously revealing the frustrations of attempting essential definitions—that is to say, attempting the highest order of definition by stating a thing's essence.

Aristotle, noted for his capacity to discern distinctions, distinguishes the beautiful from that which is simply pleasant. He cites the example of mathematical sciences as related to the beautiful by displaying the chief forms of beauty, namely, order, symmetry, and definiteness.[12] Thus, beauty is distinguishable from that which is simply pleasant or desirable, as in the desirable; the appearance of a woman. He further seems to distinguish beauty from the good in contrast to Plato by stating—"the good and the beautiful are different (for the former always implies conduct as its subject, while the beautiful is found also in motionless things)."[13] This remark, echoed by Gadamer, seems to distinguish beauty from the moral which, as we shall see, is linked by Immanuel Kant. Yet in his *Rhetoric* Aristotle states that "the beautiful is that good which is pleasant because it is good."[14] This seeming conflict in Aristotle's thought regarding the beautiful's relationship to the good appears to be acknowledged when he closes this discussion saying, "we shall speak more plainly elsewhere about these matters."[15] Such clarification by Aristotle is not found in his writings, at least not among his extant works. We do, however, come away from Aristotle with some

---

12 Aristotle, *The Basic Works of Aristotle*, trans. Richard McKeon (New York: Random House, 1941), *Metaphysics*, 893, 1078b 1–4.

13 Aristotle, *Metaphysics*, 1078a 33.

14 Aristotle, *Rhetoric*, 1345, 1366a 33–36. The Greek term *kalon* is translated noble.

15 Aristotle, *Metaphysics*, 894, 1078b 5.

specific attributes of the beautiful; again, order, symmetry, and definiteness.

Thomas Aquinas, the great appropriator of Aristotle, cannot be said to have fully developed an aesthetic and we should not attribute more to him than the brief comments he writes. Yet we do find a few remarks regarding beauty in the context of responding to the question whether goodness has the aspect of a final cause. In his question, "On Goodness in General," Aquinas states that "goodness is praised as beauty."[16] Yet the two "differ logically, for goodness properly relates to the appetite (goodness being what all things desire); and therefore it has the aspect of an end (the appetitive being a kind of movement towards a thing)."[17] He further states that,

> On the other hand, beauty relates to the cognitive faculty; for beautiful things are those which please when seen. Hence beauty consists in due proportion; for the senses delight in things duly proportioned, as in what is after their own kind—because even sense is a sort of reason, just as is every cognitive faculty.[18]

Thus, we can at least say of Aquinas's thoughts on the beautiful, as he adds elsewhere, that it includes perfection, proper proportion, and clarity,[19] and that beauty, though cognitive, cannot be fully identified with intellectual cognition nor can it be entirely reduced to apprehension of the good.

---

16 Peter Kreeft, *Summa of the Summa*, ed. Peter Kreeft (San Francisco: Ignatius Press, 1990), 93, I, 5, 4.

17 Kreeft, *Summa of the Summa*, 93, I, 5, 4, Reply Obj. 1.

18 Kreeft, *Summa of the Summa*, 93, I, 5, 4, Reply Obj. 1.

19 Kreeft, *Summa of the Summa*, I, 39, 8c.

Traversing the centuries to the early modern era, Immanuel Kant provides a brief definition of the two aesthetic judgments, namely, of the beautiful and the sublime. "The beautiful is what pleases in the mere judging of it (consequently not by intervention of any feeling of sense in accordance with a concept of the understanding). From this it follows at once that it must please apart from all interest."[20] And further he declares the beautiful as "that which, apart from a concept, is cognized as object of a *necessary* delight."[21] Nevertheless, Kant does allow for what he calls an "adherent" purpose in the beauty of, say, the functional architecture of a building or a church. Such a purpose adhering to the object of beauty makes for an impure aesthetic judgment; however, because it is not simply an expression of a feeling of satisfaction or pleasure but involves a conceptual element. His overall analysis of the beautiful focuses on four moments of taste and judgment, namely, quality, quantity, relation, and modality.[22] Kant's analysis ultimately leads him to conclude that there is some connection between aesthetics and morals, claiming that "the beautiful is the symbol of the morally good."[23] Thus, for Kant the beautiful is a subject of taste rationally discerned for contemplation and analogously associated with the morally good.

G. W. F. Hegel's understanding of beauty as something of the historical past was already alluded to earlier in this

---

20 Immanuel Kant, *Critique of Judgement* (Oxford, Oxford University Press, 2008), 97.

21 Kant, *Critique of Judgement*, 71.

22 Kant, *Critique of Judgement*. See Part I, First Section, First Book, "Analytic of the Beautiful," 35–78.

23 Kant, *Critique of Judgement*, 254.

piece.[24] Thus, we will leave him aside to further add to the list of disparate entries regarding the essential definition of nature of art and beauty. I mention even more briefly and admittedly, too briefly, the following philosophers. First, Leo Tolstoy called for art (and beauty) to only be that which evokes "those feelings that draw people towards union or already unite them" toward a utopian vision of the brotherhood of man, and it should be accessible to everyone displaying the traits of "brevity, clarity and simplicity of expression."[25] Next, John Dewey envisioned his aesthetical task as a need "to restore continuity between the refined and intensified forms of experience that are works of art."[26] He envisioned our encounter with art and the beautiful as an experience evoking certain feelings. He adds later that the "esthetic experience is imaginative" and that "all experience has of necessity some degree of imaginative quality."[27]

Then there is the phenomenologist, Martin Heidegger, who attempted a new beginning for aesthetics by going back to Being of all beings. He declares the

> Being of all beings is what is most seemly (*das Scheinendste*)—that is, what is most beautiful, what is most beautiful, what is most constant in itself. What the Greeks meant by "beauty" is discipline. The gathering together of the highest contending is *polemos*, struggle in the sense of

---

[24] For further description of Hegel's depiction of beauty and its relationship to his overall speculative philosophy, see my previously mentioned paper, "Beauty Will Save the World"—And Education? *Journal of Faith and the Academy*, Vol. XI, No. 2, Fall 2018.

[25] Leo Tolstoy, *What is Art?*, trans. Richard Pevear and Larissa Volokhonsky (London: Penguin Books, 1995), 156.

[26] John Dewey, *Art as Experience* (New York: The Penguin Group, 2005), 2.

[27] Dewey, *Art as Experience*, 283.

confrontation, the setting-apart-from-each-other (*Aus-ein-ander-setzung*). In contrast, for us today, the beautiful is the relaxing, what is restful and thus intended for enjoyment.[28]

We could say Heidegger's estimation of our relationship to art and the beautiful, is that we have become lazy by reducing the challenge and unsettling nature of art and beauty's "setting-apart-from-each-other" to something of ease and to diversionary entertainment.

To conclude this brief overview of a few select authors' attempts at defining or describing art and the beautiful, I point to the author, Roger Scruton, and his nuanced treatment of aesthetics in his book, *Beauty*. In response to whether beauty has an objective property, he exclaims in his concluding thoughts, "everything I have said about the experience of beauty implies that it is rationally founded."[29] That is to say, he claims that while certainly there is the subjective element involved in one's encounter with the beautiful, there is, nevertheless, the experience of the beautiful is rationally grounded. As well, Scruton affirms the cross-cultural and historically continuous universals of the objective traits of beauty, specifically, "symmetry, order, proportion, closure, convention, harmony, and also novelty and excitement,"[30] which echoes our earlier voices from antiquity. Scruton then

---

28 Martin Heidegger, *Introduction to Metaphysics*, trans. Gregory Fried and Richard Polt (New Haven, CT: Yale University Press, 2000), 140.

29 Roger Scruton, *Beauty: A Very Short Introduction* (Oxford: Oxford University Press, 2009), 197.

30 Scruton, *Beauty*, 142. These characteristics of beauty we see echoed by Plato and Aristotle as well as others making for a bit of a consensus.

adds, "all these [traits] seem to have a permanent hold on the human psyche."[31]

The conundrum in all these entries to define or at least circumscribe beauty is the problem of seeking the ideal definition, that is, a definition of essences. Other forms of definition include nominal (definition of the word rather than the thing), definition by properties, by accidents, by final cause, by material cause, and by effects.[32] Concerning the beautiful we bump into the limitations of definition, namely, the definition of essences. Just as Being cannot be defined in its essence because it does not fit into any category and is a universal, so too with the transcendental, traditionally listed as something being (materially existing), such as the one, true, good, and beautiful.[33] Thus, we are limited to defining the beautiful by way of its properties, accidents, or effects. Nevertheless, it is a noble task to make the attempt at defining the transcendentals in their essences, as long as we realize we are spitting into the metaphysical wind.

Wonder as a Means of Recovering Beauty

Now to the questions of what can be done to recover and discover beauty in our lives. The first step is to look with the eyes of a child at the world in wonder. Allow me to share a personal example. During a walk in the woods last fall, I saw a small object lying within the fallen leaves and it immediate-

---

31 Scruton, *Beauty*, 142.

32 Peter Kreeft, *Socratic Logic*, 3.1 ed. (South Bend, IN: St. Augustine Press: 2014), 125.

33 Kreeft, *Socratic Logic*, 130.

ly caught my attention. Initially I thought it was a piece of jewelry, a broach perhaps, accidentally dropped by some fellow walker. I stooped to pick it up and behold. A moth! A Harnessed Tiger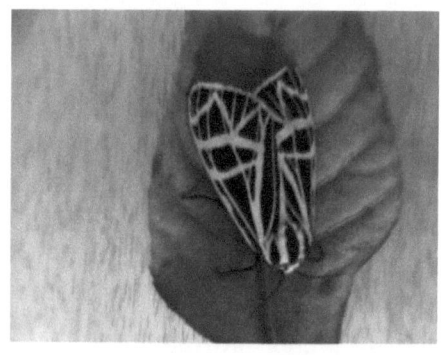
Moth, to be specific. It so clearly stood out among all the leaves with its intricate design and almost iridescent crisp lines. What I thought was a shiny manmade piece of jewelry was a beautifully created bug! I marveled at its beauty and held it in captivated wonder. I have since shown it to others and the consistent response has been, "Oh, wow!"

But what do we mean by "wonder" and what is its relationship to beauty? We return briefly to Immanuel Kant to hear his comments on the sublime and to detect the connection between beauty, the sublime, and wonder. The sublime, he asserts, is "what pleases immediately through its resistance to the interest of the senses."[34] Kant allows for and enumerates the agreements between the beautiful and the sublime, such as both are pleasing on their own account and stir reflection.[35] Yet the two are distinguishable in that the beautiful is "a presentation of an indeterminate concept of the understanding" whereas the sublime is "of an independent concept of reason."[36] I would simply add to this conception of the sublime to connect it to or to allow it to fall within the

---

34 Kreeft, *Socratic Logic*, 97.

35 Kreeft, *Socratic Logic*, 75.

36 Kreeft, *Socratic Logic*, 75.

sense of wonder, and that is, it evokes a sense of awe. Wonder leaves one speechless and captivated by the object. Wonder causes us to marvel over the mystery of what is before us; it physically stands before us and yet we acknowledge that it is something more.

Thomas Dubay's book, *The Evidential Power of Beauty: Science and Theology Meet*, helps us see more wondrous things during a walk in the woods beyond our moth and with greater detail. I cite just a couple of marvels from nature; or as Dubay classifies them, macromarvels, midmarvels, and micromarvels. An example of a macromarvel: our sun burns four million tons of its own substance every second, yet over the next six billion years it will consume only one forty-thousandth of its mass.[37] A couple of midmarvels: one, the Blackpoll warbler migrates from Nova Scotia to South America over four days and nights, a 2,400 mile trek with the fuel-efficiency rate comparable to 720,000 miles per gallon.[38] And this: it is noted that in proportion to the wattage of a bat's 'radar' it is millions of times more effective than man-made radar or sonar.[39] Maybe we should not be so overly impressed with man's current technology. Then there is this micromarvel: water, the source for all life. There have been over one hundred different theories put forth to try and depict how it behaves the way it does, yet none provide a fully accurate explanation.[40] And there is the recognized paradox of light. As

---

[37] Thomas Dubay, *The Evidential Power of Beauty: Science and Theology Meet* (San Francisco: Ignatius Press, 1999), 136.

[38] Dubay, *The Evidential Power of Beauty*, 158.

[39] Dubay, *The Evidential Power of Beauty*, 158.

[40] Dubay, *The Evidential Power of Beauty*, 167. This is an indication of the anthropic principle which points to the crafting or fine-tuning of the universe to sustain and support life and human life in particular.

Einstein came to realize, light is both particle and wave at the same time. The two contrasting descriptors of light together only capture a portion of the mystery of light because we do not know how light can be both at the same time. It must be something more.

We turn from beauty found in nature and its power to evoke our sense of wonder to the beauty of art created by man. The beauty of nature begets beauty through our imitation, expression, and the sharing of beauty in all forms of artwork; painting, sculpture, architecture, music, and literature. These manmade forms of art serve as images that help put us in touch with the divine. Thomas Pfau's recent work, *Incomprehensible Certainty: Metaphysics and Hermeneutics of the Image*, is interested in how images influence the way we see the world.[41] Drawing upon Maurice Merleau-Ponty, Pfau argues that one does not just see images, but one sees according to them: images we spend time with become a lens through which we see the rest of the world.[42] This implies that if we spend time with ugly images we will tend to see the ugly in the world and the world as ugly. If we spend time with beautiful images, we will tend toward seeing beauty around us and that the world is beautiful. Thus, beautiful artistic images have the beneficent power to call us to a more complete vision of reality. Beautiful artwork or images can teach us to see in an awe-struck way. "Rightly seen, visible things reveal invisible, numinous depths, a fecund excess that spills out into the visible world and calls us to a more vital, contemplative, mor-

---

41 Thomas Pfau, *Incomprehensible Certainty: Metaphysics and Hermeneutics of the Image* (South Bend, IN: University of Notre Dame Press, 2022).

42 Paraphrased from Mark Spencer's book review of *Incomprehensible Certainty* in the online journal, "The Power of Images." Law & Liberty, Dec. 27, 2022.

al, and religious life."[43] Thus, the power of beautiful objects can manifest or unveil a depth and a splendor that moves us toward wonder; a longing for something higher and greater. And to be in wonder causes us to want to speak and to share our encounters with the beautiful. As Pfau proclaims, "visible beauty calls for spoken beauty."[44] Hence, the literary corpus of beautiful writing to be found in poetry, novels, and stories. Nature, artwork, images, literature, music, architecture all hold the potential to reveal a beauty and wonder that opens up a glimmer of the beauty of God.

> One thing I asked the Lord,
> that will I seek after:
> to live in the house of the Lord
> all the days of my life,
> to behold the beauty of the Lord,
> and to inquire in his temple.
>
> - Psalm 27:4

Conclusion

I conclude with a cautionary note about beauty's power to also distract us. James M. Kushiner, editor of *Touchstone: Journal of Mere Christianity*, notes:

> [...]our experience of beauty and our response to it may or may not serve the Gospel, just as our experiences of joy, ecstasy, joy, longing, guilt, grief, sorrow, sickness, and war

---

43 Spencer, "The Power of Images."

44 Pfau, *Incomprehensible Certainty*.

may or may not point us in the direction of healing and salvation. Beauty may attract or distract us.[45]

Nevertheless, even with Kushiner's wise caution of beauty's capacity to distract us from God and that our perverted wills tend to idolize it, we can still confidently affirm that beauty holds the power to inspire us and awaken us to the presence of God in His creation and through our attempts to capture such beauty in images of all forms of artwork. So where has all the beauty gone? It is still all around us. It is a constituent element of all creation, a dynamic running throughout and through-in the cosmos. It is a way of seeing, understanding, being, and living with the truth of things. Attending to the reality of the beautiful within the world and through art is a movement from a hermeneutic of suspicion to a hermeneutic of wonder. If nothing else, at least take a walk in the woods and see.

☐

Michael R. Young graduated from Abilene Christian University with a BS, MS, and an MDiv and attained an MA, PhD in philosophy from the University of Dallas as well as a certification in Spiritual Direction from Spring Hill College. Dr. Young is a professor of philosophy in Faulkner University's doctoral Humanities program and an adjunct professor in Johnson University's doctoral Christian Leadership program. He serves as an editor for the *Journal of Faith and the Academy* and the *Stone-Campbell Journal*.

Dr. Young is married to Carla, an architect. They have four children and five grandchildren.

---

[45] James M. Kushiner, editorial comments in *Fellow of St. James*, www.fsj.org, October, 24, 2017.

The Beautiful Art of Brokenness

A Review of Rembrandt is in the Wind by Russ Ramsey

by Sarah Abbott, MA

Ramsey, Russ. *Rembrandt is in the wind: Learning to love art through the eyes of faith*. Grand Rapids, MI: Zondervan Reflective, 2022, hardcover, $21.49, 256 pp.

About five years ago I learned that I love art. Not long after, I began to see that artists were more than just the art they illustrated, but real people with their own complicated lives, often filled with turmoil and heartache, as well as vision and joy. Since I already eagerly sought out opportunities to learn about art, discovering this meaningful relationship between the artists' stories and their work gave me comforting insight into my own multifaceted life experiences.

Because learning about art and the lives of artists has had such a profound impact on my own faith journey, I am always on the lookout for books that help people view art in connection with a richer understanding of the Christian faith. *Rembrandt is in the Wind: Learning to Love Art Through the Eyes of Faith*, by Russ Ramsey is just that kind of book. Ramsey, a Presbyterian pastor living in Tennessee, has clearly been deeply impacted by the art world as well. In describing how this originated, he writes, "In high school, I had the good fortune of having an art teacher who loved art. She wanted us to love it too, so she introduced us not only to the great works of art but, more importantly, to the people who created them."[1]

Ramsey compels readers to appreciate more than just the stunning art depicted in this book. He does not simply write about time periods, techniques, and styles used by the artists; instead he presents us with a book about beauty so that we cannot help but catch a glimmer of transcendent beauty, not only through art, but also through brokenness. By transporting us into the lives of the nine different artists described in *Rembrandt is in the Wind*, Ramsey offers us a rich portrayal of beauty through the stories he tells, teaches us to appreciate the genuine value of brokenness, and leaves us pondering deeply challenging questions of these real people who, in many ways, mirror our own lives.

Ramsey devotes the first chapter to describing beauty: what it is, how we unknowingly long for it, and why the world so desperately needs it. This picture of beauty is portrayed alongside goodness and truth, the three-fold transcendentals that, in their purest forms, reside in God, Himself. Ramsey defines beauty as that which "elevates and gives pleasure to the mind and senses."[2] While it is an essential human need however, we often opt for inferior substitutes by devoting our attention to what is easy, utilitarian, and mundane. The unconscious hunger for beauty drives people to visit the ocean,

---

1   Russ Ramsey, *Rembrandt is in the Wind: Learning to Love Art Through the Eyes of Faith* (Grand Rapids, MI: Zondervan Reflective, 2022) 213.

2   Ramsey, *Rembrandt is in the Wind*, 7.

amble through museums, and gaze at the stars in an effort to be captivated by beauty. When we do encounter a glimpse of transcendent beauty, it compels us to lift our eyes beyond the visible to the God who created. Ramsey furnishes us with this opportunity through the stories he tells.

In the chapter entitled "Pursuing Perfection," Ramsey tells us three stories that collectively reveal an intricately woven example of beauty: the artist Michelangelo, the stone he shaped, and the shepherd he depicted. First, we learn about Michelangelo, his cherished childhood where his love of sculpture was born, and his character as a man full of passion. He was fascinated with beauty, devoted to God, and yet enslaved by sensual desires. Then we read the story of the massive piece of marble out of which Michelangelo carved the seventeen-foot tall statue of David. Readers discover that the discarded block of stone lay waiting for a craftsman like Michelangelo for forty years. Finally, Ramsey unites the stories of the artist and the stone together with the subject of the sculpture, David the shepherd king. David was as complex as Michelangelo. He was a man of passion who loved God deeply but also battled, and succumbed to his fleshly desires at times as well. As Ramsey patiently develops each of these three stories and then weaves them together as one, readers discover more than just the background of the sculpture of David but most assuredly gain eye-opening insight into our own humanity that is similarly beautiful and broken.

As with Michelangelo, Ramsey continues to carefully depict each of the artists' in the book by walking readers through their lives and the art they created while emphasizing how brokenness can lead to the beautiful. One such example is the well-known Vincent Van Gogh, the Dutch Post-Impressionist painter who lived in the mid-1800s. Sadly,

Van Gogh was a deeply troubled man who ultimately surrendered to despair by taking his own life. While Van Gogh was obsessed with capturing beauty, which was evident in the amount of paintings he produced in a short amount of time, he never hid who he was. In fact, one of his most famous self-portraits is *Self-Portrait with Bandaged Ear*, an illustration of himself painted after he had cut off his own ear. The complicated life of such an incredibly talented and deeply tortured artist reminds readers that God sees us, as Ramsey explains, "fully exposed in our shortcomings, yet...of unimaginable value to him."[3]

The idea that our brokenness can reveal transcendent beauty is only one of the challenging concepts this book leaves readers to grapple with. I had never heard of Lilias Trotter before reading *Rembrandt is in the Wind*. A contemporary of famous artists like Van Gogh, Gauguin, and Renoir, Lilias was an incredibly talented watercolorist. Thanks to her mother, she was discovered by the highly regarded writer and artist John Ruskin, who, after seeing her work, believed he could make her famous. Ruskin impressed upon Lilias that, in order for her to be the artist she had the potential to be, she must devote herself entirely to developing her artistic talents under his direction. While Lilias loved to paint, she longed to help the poor and spread the Gospel more. Therefore, much to Ruskin's great disappointment, Lilias made the decision to become a missionary in Algeria. While she was confident in her decision to serve God, Lilias still grieved the loss of her art for the remainder of her life.

---

3 Ramsey, *Rembrandt is in the Wind*, 5.

The Beautiful Art of Brokenness

Lilias's story is only one of the stories in *Rembrandt is in the Wind* that leaves readers facing perplexing questions about beauty and brokenness. When we meet Vincent Van Gogh on these pages, we are grieved and confounded as we ask why he took his own life. As we read Edward Hopper's story we question how artistic depictions of loneliness lead to encountering beauty. Moreover, when reading about Caravaggio, we cannot help but question how someone as remarkably gifted as he was, when portraying biblical truth on a canvas, could live such a degenerate and duplicitous life. Within this book there are still more stories, more depictions of the profound unity between beauty and brokenness, and more questions to be asked about human nature and the divine, brilliantly displayed for readers.

I will never forget the time, several years ago, when I was driving across the vast state of Montana in my sister's old green pick-up truck with my son. In front of us, visible through a bug-splattered windshield, rose the Grand Teton mountains. Encountering their astounding beauty for the first time gripped my heart in a way that brought me to tears. While I could not adequately express what I was seeing, I had to praise God for His glorious creation that shocked me with its awe-inspiring beauty. This is the only way I know how to relate my understanding of discovering the transcendent beauty Ramsey describes so well in *Rembrandt is in the Wind*. Ramsey's love of art and the attentiveness he has taken to carefully share the artists' stories offers readers a compassionate portrayal of the complexity of humanity. To read a book in which the author understands that people are made in the image of God, yet broken by this sin-filled world and somehow still beautiful, is special and absolutely worth reading again and again.

THE CONSORTIUM

☐

Sarah Abbott is a native of Massachusetts and has been a teacher, curriculum writer, coach, and administrator for people of all ages for over twenty-five years. She holds a BA in Elementary Education and an MA in Education. She currently serves as the co-founder of the Classical Learning Consortium for New England.

Vast Beauty and Staggering Wonder

Putting the Childlike Spirit Back into Education

by Junius Johnson, PhD

"For repose is not the end of education; its end is a noble unrest, an ever renewed awaking from the dead, a ceaseless questioning of the past for the interpretation of the future, an urging on of the motions of life, which had better far be accelerated into fever, than retarded into lethargy."[1] Thus does George MacDonald, in beginning an essay about the imagination, start with education. I would like to suggest that we could do worse, in our philosophy of education, than to turn MacDonald around and start with the imagination.

There are three connected aspects of the life of a rational creature: wonder, beauty, and imagination. The imagination is a faculty; beauty is an experience; wonder is a response. All three of these breathe with unrestrained exuberance in the heart and mind of a child; all three find themselves constrained and abandoned to various degrees in the hearts of most adults. This is the reality of our experience in the world: what are we to do with it when it comes to education?

---

1   George MacDonald, "The Imagination: Its Functions and Its Culture," in *A Dish of Orts* (London: Sampson Low, Marston, & Co. 1893), 2–3.

The Centrality of the Mindset of the Child

To begin with, the child's state, not the adult's state, should be normative for education. Adults sometimes learn things, but learning is not native to that stage of life. This is because learning has to do with growing, while adulthood is concerned not with growing, but the judicious application of the things grown. That loaded word "maturity," which is a double-edged sword, means that a thing has reached the fullness of its form. The mature fruit has reached its final form in the sense that it is as complete an expression of the idea of that fruit as it will ever be. It has become as perfect as it has the power to be. It will go on changing, but that change is now no longer towards ever-better instantiation of the essence of mango; now it is putrescence, as it declines from that central perfection towards its actual *telos*, which is to give its life that another may live, and so become the seed of many more like itself.

This is a rich metaphor, but applied to humans, it leaves us with a paradigm whereby the person has finished the educational process when he or she arrives at adulthood, at maturity. We go from a stance fundamentally characterized by learning to one fundamentally characterized by knowing.

Children, by contrast, are always learning things, from the first moment of their emergence until the heavy mantle of adulthood settles upon them. It is native to their state, for wonder and the search for beauty are natural to childhood, and these are also the engine of learning.

Now, this does not mean that adults don't learn, because no adult is only an adult. As C. S. Lewis says, "humanity does not pass through phases as a train passes through stations:

being alive, it has the privilege of always moving yet never leaving anything behind. Whatever we have been, in some sort we are still."[2] If Lewis is right, we do not lose our childhood when we become adults: we just gain a complicated relationship to it, a relationship we must negotiate, because we can never get out of it. So then, adults are teachable just to the extent that they are not *only* adults, but also still the children they once were. This is what makes wonder so very special: we come back to it after 40 or 50 years of life, and find that it has not changed: it still feels like it did when we were 6.

The Greeks probably called what they did *paedogogia* ("child-leading") because it was about making children into proper adults: they were to become good citizens of the *polis*, and the process was complete when they were prepared to set aside being children and take an adult role in the common life. The notion of education as a process that has a *telos* that is also a *terminus*, a place at which one ends, is infelicitous. But the word-image of "child-leading" is fortuitous, because it underscores that every learner, whatever his age, is led by the part of his soul that is childlike.

That means that when we look to define our philosophy of education and our values in learning, we should look to the experts: children. The childlike experience of learning should be the ground of our educational design. Only we must always remember the important distinction between the childlike and the childish, which C. S. Lewis encapsulates so well in his essay "On Three Ways of Writing for Children:"

> Critics who treat 'adult' as a term of approval, instead of as a merely descriptive term, cannot be adult themselves. To

---

2   C. S. Lewis, *The Allegory of Love* (Oxford: Oxford University Press, 1936), 1.

> be concerned about being grown up, to admire the grown up because it is grown up, to blush at the suspicion of being childish; these things are the marks of childhood and adolescence. [...] When I was ten, I read fairy tales in secret and would have been ashamed if I had been found doing so. Now that I am fifty I read them openly. When I became a man I put away childish things, including the fear of childishness and the desire to be very grown up.[3]

Freedom from childishness is the prerequisite for childlikeness. Children are not childlike, they are *actually children*. And so the disposition that will come to be called "childlike" in adults is native to them; but it is simultaneous with a childishness that is not yet blameworthy, because it is not yet out of place.

This is where curricular design that is "child-led" often goes wrong: it fails to distinguish the childlike from the childish. The former is proper to childhood, yet necessary for the fullness of maturity; the latter is proper to childhood, and impairs maturity. The adult, not the child, is best suited to note where the line of this distinction falls: and so curricular design must not be child-led, but rather child-leading (*paedogogia*); nevertheless, we lead them by their loves.

---

3   C. S. Lewis, "On Three Ways of Writing for Children," in *On Stories and Other Essays on Literature*, ed. Walter Hooper (San Diego: Harvest Books, 1982), 34.

How Children Learn: Wonder, Beauty, and Imagination

How then do children learn? They learn by following wonder and beauty, and they follow these by means of the imagination.

Wonder

According to Aristotle, philosophy begins in wonder.[4] Commenting on this idea, Thomas Aquinas says "when we see certain obvious effects whose cause we don't know, we wonder about their cause."[5] What Aristotle and Aquinas are pointing to is an intellectual gap that gives rise to the experience of wonder: I see that I do not know why something is the case, and so there is room for me to investigate. This is an intellectual sort of wonder. It is like saying: "I wonder if it will rain?" Such wonder is important, because without it the student will not be driven to ask "why" questions, which are the heart of learning.

But there is another sort of wonder. I am tempted to say that it is wonder of the imagination, but I think even that is too small (it is only that the imagination is the faculty best suited for laying hold of it). It is the wonder of the soul: it takes up all of our faculties, indeed all of who we are, and

---

4   "For it is owing to their wonder that men both now begin and at first began to philosophize [...] and a man who is puzzled and wonders thinks himself ignorant." Aristotle, *Metaphysics*, in *The Complete Works of Aristotle*, volume 2, ed. Jonathan Barnes (Princeton, NJ: Princeton University Press, 1984), 982b12–18.

5   Thomas Aquinas, *Commentary on Aristotle's Metaphysics*, trans. John P. Rowan (Notre Dame, IN: Dumb Ox Books, 1961), Book One, III.55, 19.

so it cannot even be limited to the soul, but also sweeps our bodies along too. Our entire being vibrates with this wonder, resonating to a mighty note that not only fills our ears, but commandeers our very heartbeats as well.

This wonder has in common with intellectual wonder the recognition of great disparity. But it is not only or primarily a disparity of understanding. It is rather a disparity of *being*. When we are caught up into this kind of wonder, we are awestruck by the greatness or smallness of creation, by the amplitude of beauty, by the surpassing *more*ness of God. There is something numinous in every such experience of wonder, even when it is aroused by very natural things. This wonder is born of the realization, recognition, or remembrance of the fact that the world is a magical place.

This is the most fertile ground for education because it is the most fertile ground for learning. The heart captivated by wonder knows that the right response is to stay open, to remain in the place of wonder so that we may receive as much of the miracle as possible. We see this also in our Lord: Jesus taught by signs and wonders because he knew that the wonders would break up the fallow ground of complacent hearts and render them rich and loamy.

Beauty

I have argued elsewhere that beauty is that which reminds us of God.[6] Any time we find something beautiful, it is activating a memory that we may not even be aware we have of the Creator and exemplar of all things. It is specifically

---

6 Junius Johnson, *The Father of Lights: A Theology of Beauty* (Grand Rapids, MI: Baker Academic, 2020), 21.

Christ to whom this experience is referenced, who is himself the first image and complete expression of the power of the Father. Beauty excites our Christological longing and summons us towards the fount and goal of our being.

Beauty therefore has an inherently referential character. The whole purpose and the very nature of the experience of beauty is to guide the mind from the thing experienced as beautiful to the very ground of beauty. Thus beauty is inherently educational, for it leads the mind from recognition of the excellence of this thing to the awareness of more excellent things.

So, when I present students with beauty, I do not have to motivate a journey for them: if they recognize it as beautiful, they are already on a journey. What remains to me is to guide that journey, to point out singular things along the way, other beauties that will continue to spur the students on. Chesterton says: "one elephant having a trunk was odd; but all elephants having trunks looked like a plot."[7] In a similar way, the consistent and ubiquitous presence of beauty in the educational journey will crystallize in the student's mind into the conviction that they have uncovered a plot. Something is afoot, and they intend to get to the bottom of it. At this point, I rather have to hold them back than spur them on.

One of the great things about beauty is that you don't have to present an argument for it, or convince the students that they should value it. They may need help to see that something is beautiful, but once they have seen that, their allegiance is automatic. Beauty needs no apologetic because we are hard-wired for it. As creatures, we were not only made

---

[7] G. K. Chesterton, "The Ethics of Elfland," in *Orthodoxy* (New York, Image Books, 1959), 57.

to be beautiful, but made to be with a beautiful God, the one who is the source, referent, and goal of all beauty. Every human heart understands this, regardless of its religious disposition and cultural sophistication. We can only dim, not eradicate, our allegiance to beauty.

An Unfettered Imagination

My daughter's kindergarten class has rules for coloring. I saw them for the first time when I went for a routine parent-teacher conference. At first, it seemed quite innocuous: "color within the lines." But then I saw the rule: "use appropriate colors." There may even have been an example, such as "the sun should not be blue." From my side, my wife immediately said "I don't know that I like that." I nodded.

The situation is complicated. The problem is not that kids should not be taught to render the world in ways that are mimetic; they should. The problem is that, in doing so, we run the risk of telling them it is not okay to do otherwise.

If the goal is to draw a picture of our world, it is probably right to use appropriate colors. But this is only probably right: for our world is many-layered and multi-faceted. It cannot be exhaustively represented by how it appears to unimpaired vision. For that reason, sometimes we may want to use surprising colors, colors that are factually false, in order to get at a deeper truth.

But depicting our world is not the only art I want my daughter to do. I also want her to draw other worlds, to take me to the places only she can see, and in so doing to help me out of myself (an inherent good) and into her mind (a parental good). And if the goal is to draw other worlds, we have no basis for saying what colors are appropriate. Just because our sun is not blue does not mean I do not want to think about worlds where the sun *is* blue.

I understood what the teacher was trying to teach, and had no wish to undermine it. Mimetic or factual learning is an important part of any education, and especially classical education. There are facts of the matter about the world, and knowledge remains, in a real sense, an adequation of the knower to the thing known.[8] All building of other worlds must be founded in true knowledge of this one. How then, to put together the necessity of *mimesis* with the desire for intellectual and imaginative *play*?

Well, I simply told my daughter: "when you are at school, use appropriate colors. But in your own art, don't be afraid to imagine other realities." She is used to this kind of double-standard: it is like when she came home and told me that (a different) teacher had told her that unicorns were not real. I responded that just because she could not meet them in our world did not mean they were not real. A week later, she had stopped asking whether things were real; she now asks instead whether something is real in *our* world. She has not lost the distinction between the factual and the fantastical, which is what some fear; she has not lost her love of the fantastical, which is what I fear; and she has not lost her curiosity about the world we actually live in. See how easily the mind of the child holds all realities, whatever their facticity, together!

What I am concerned about here are fetters for the imagination. Too often we think that in order to correctly encounter the world as it is given to us, we must bind our imaginations to the forms we find it in. But this is false: we

---

8 Thomas Aquinas, *On Truth*, question 1, article 1, response.

cannot correctly interpret this world without going beyond appearances. This is as true physically (think of subatomic particles, quantum fields, and dark matter) as it is spiritually. The world is so much more than it seems.

A priori boundaries for the imagination arise from and convey the notion of certainty. We say to the students: "Look no further in this direction; we've been down that road, and it doesn't go anywhere." Then we wonder why they turn in papers that are uninspired and unoriginal. They learned it from us.

The reality is that our hard-won certainties are always provisional at best. I cannot imagine anything useful down that path; but why should humanity be limited to only what I can imagine, when I am a very finite and incomplete creature? A large part of the point of having billions of humans is because no one, or ten, or ten million humans could exhaust the human ways of seeing the world. I must leave open the possibility that one of my students will be equipped to find what I cannot, to go where I cannot.

Jesus said: "A disciple is not above his teacher, but everyone when he is fully trained will be like his teacher."[9] Is this not proof that what I am looking for is something the students cannot deliver? They cannot go beyond me because that is not how teacher-student relationships work: the best they can hope for is to be like me? But just before this, Jesus said: "Can a blind man lead a blind man? Will they not both fall into a pit?"[10] His point is that you cannot give what you do not have. We must not universalize this: if no student could go beyond his teacher, human knowledge would never

---

9   Luke 6:40.

10 Luke 6:39.

progress. It must, then, not be enough for the student to be like the teacher; she must be able to be more. We do this by not limiting their imaginations to only the things we thought were possible.

But how do we do that? Jesus has already shown us. Our students will be like us, not in knowledge, but in *training*. If we allow provisional certainties to calcify into rigid restrictions, we will train them up into the same failure of imagination that has set a limit to our own understanding. We must continually practice unfettering our imaginations so that we may, as much as is possible for us, avoid placing the same shackles on our students. Only imaginative teachers will have imaginative students.

☐

Dr. Junius Johnson is an independent scholar, teacher, musician, writer, and the executive director of Junius Johnson Academics. He holds a BA from Oral Roberts University, a Master of Arts in Religion from Yale Divinity School, and an MA, two MPhils, and a PhD from Yale University. He is the author of four books, including *The Father of Lights: A Theology of Beauty*. He is married to Rebekah and resides in Memphis, TN.

Review of *Mr. Bliss* by J. R. R. Tolkien

by Christy Anne Vaughan, EdD

Tolkien, J. R. R. *Mr. Bliss*. HarperCollins, 2011, hardcover, $18.95, 192 pp.

While not as expansive in plot or intricate in narrative as Tolkien's more celebrated works such as *The Hobbit* or *The Lord of the Rings*, Mr. Bliss overflows with whimsy and silliness in a sweet, bedtime story type of way. It is written as a simple, funny fantasy to be read to small children (Amazon.com suggests ages 2–6). Similar in style to the earlier published adventures of a young Alice, it is not as dark (characters who are "mad," smoking a hookah, or exhibiting an unhealthy and unreasonable fear of being late) or violent as Lewis Carroll's *Alice's Adventures in Wonderland*. While Tolkien intended this book to rival Carroll's *Alice*, *Mr. Bliss* did not receive as warm a welcome. The publisher's dust jacket notes that Tolkien's hand drawn illustrations were considered too expensive to publish. Thankfully, his heirs and publisher HarperCollins put the book into print recently in 2011, complete with Tolkien's handwritten version of the story. Text and illustrative drawings take up a slim seventy five pages. Interestingly, the publisher chose to publish the original in landscape view immediately after the typeset version in portrait style. In effect, the printing style is as quirky as the book itself.

The adventures follow a strangely dressed Mr. Bliss through several adventures, complete with recognizable characters as well as the fantastical. Puns and aptronym (naming a character based on appearance) abound as they often do in children's tales and allegorical stories. There are both motorcars and horse drawn carts, lovely gardens and bustling towns, tensions destroying relationships and friendships built. The only romance is alluded to and ends well. The adventures are not scary, although some danger is realized by the characters, but no one is eaten and no one is seriously injured. The scariest characters are called bears but drawn as the stuffed Teddy variety. After a dust-up, the characters usually end up amicably having tea or dinner together. It is written in the British style and vernacular, with a few lines from one character in the Cockney dialect similar to those found in *My Fair Lady/Pygmalion*. Also, the book sports unusual and questionable punctuation (single quotation marks, no period after Mr and Mrs in the text). Grammar purists may not approve.

All-in-all it is a delightful read and well worth the time. I asked a few students to read it and one found it too short, but funny. She especially liked the Girabbit, introduced on page fifteen. I do not believe that one can find details of the adventures of a Girabbit outside the pages of this book. Worth the purchase price indeed.

Review of Mr. Bliss by J. R. R. Tolkien

Dr. Christy Vaughan holds an EdD from Liberty University in Educational Leadership and serves as Secretary for Classical Christian Education International, Inc. (www.2CEI.ORG) and is homeschooling two of her grandchildren in Ohio. She has more than ten years of experience in public and private education in both online and brick-and-mortar classrooms, and she currently offers courses in preparation for a career in Christian education through Kepler Education.

The Aesthetics of Humility

by Gregory Soderberg, PhD

The questions: "What is poetry, music, art?" "How can they not be?" "How do they act upon us and how do we interpret their action?" are, ultimately, theological questions.

- George Steiner, *Real Presences*

I will show the things that are now being done,
And some of the things that were long ago done,
That you may take heart. Make perfect your will.
Let me show you the work of the humble. Listen.

- T. S. Eliot, *Choruses From "The Rock"*

Introduction

There are many reasons for the decay of the arts in the last two centuries. Christian thinkers such as Francis Schaeffer, Hans Rookmaaker, Gene Edward Veith, Leland Ryken, and Ken Myers have forced Christians to look seriously at this situation. There are also many Christian artists who are beginning to apply their faith to their art. However, many well-meaning Christians never get beyond appealing to the Bible in aesthetic discussions and then falling back on what amounts to a plea for "traditional values." Christians *should* quote the Bible, not because they do not understand modern art, but because they understand it better than modernists and postmodernists do. In fact, the unbelieving artist cannot really understand what he is doing (Ro. 1:21–22), except through God's common grace. But Christians can do more than simply show the modern artist how fragmented and ugly his art is. After telling the artist to submit humbly to God we must provide concrete applications.

This paper will take one cardinal virtue in Scripture, namely *humility*, and use it as a window into the arts. There are several reasons for approaching aesthetics through the virtue of humility. First, this is how all genuine knowledge and enquiry must proceed: in humble submission to God. Second, it is easy to get lost in the twists and turns of aesthetic theory. Everyone has an opinion, and without a theological attitude of humility, the whole project can seem pointless. We don't have to refute Kant and Hegel immediately. It is enough to humbly seek God's wisdom on the matter, and let the rest fall into place. Thirdly, other Christian thinkers have already thought much on humility and the arts, and we would spurn our inheritance if we did not consult them before rushing off to fight the modern dragons. Finally, a community of Christian artists working in humble submission to God is the best argument we can provide, and the best antidote to postmodern ugliness.

I sympathize with Thomas Eakins when he says, "About the philosophy of aesthetics, to be sure we do not greatly concern ourselves, but we are considerably concerned with learning how to paint."[1] Jorge Luis Borges also has some healthy views on aesthetic theories: "After so many—too many—years of practicing literature, I do not profess any aesthetic. Why add to the natural limits which habit imposes on us, those of some theory or other?"[2] In another place he says, "I don't believe in any aesthetic theories. In general, they are little more than useless abstractions; they vary with each writer and each text, and can be no more than occasional stimulants or instruments."[3]

While aesthetic speculation can be a helpful pursuit, its *telos* must be *homo*, as well as *theo*, centric. All things must be done to the glory of God, but all things must also be done for the edification of the brethren (1 Cor. 14:26). Jacques Maritain provides a good illustration of the different ends involved in the artistic situation: "Not only is our act of artistic creation ordered to an ultimate end, true God or false God, but it is impossible that it not regard, because of the environment in which it steeps, certain proximate ends that concern the human order."[4] One criteria of an aesthetic theory's worth should be how it affects these "proximate ends."

Humility not only provides a metaphysical framework for the artist, but it also gives us an operational procedure for synthesizing the proximate ends of the art-situation. There is no single "method" for producing great art. Nor should Christians eager for reformation draw up a manifesto. The

---

1 Robert Goldwater and Marco Treves, eds., *Artists on Art* (New York: Pantheon, 1970), 355.

2 Jorge Luis Borges, *Selected Poems*, ed. Alexander Coleman (New York: Viking, 1999), 345.

3 Borges, *Selected Poems*, 265.

4 Jacques Maritain, *Art and Scholasticism* (New York: Charles Scribner's Sons, 1962), 73.

situation is more organic, as in the human frame or the Church, where there are many parts, but one body.

In the particular situation of the arts there are three elements, each of which has its own proximate ends, which must be considered: 1) Artist, 2) Audience, 3) Artwork. In every art situation I can think of, these three elements exist. Painting: painter, painting, observer. Literature: author, work, reader. Theater: author, play, audience. Music: composer, music, audience. The last two situations are complicated by the fact that performers must mediate the work to the audience. In a sense, they are both creative and passive in this mediatorial capacity. They both actively interpret the work, and passively let the work affect them. They are both artists and audience. But although groups or individuals may act in dual aesthetic roles, the basic structure remains the same.

In other areas, such as cooking, plumbing, automobile-repair, we find the same pattern. The cook prepares food, which is consumed by others. The mechanic works on a car, which is evaluated by the owner. A simplified equation would be: producer, product, consumer. But the point is not to reduce the arts to economics. My point is that there is a basic pattern which man, as an agent of transformation, must follow. Applied to the arts, this gives us a framework of *considerations*, not a paint-by-numbers kit. When the virtue of humility is added, we have the potential for a godly art situation.

Each element of this three-fold structure illustrates the problem of the one and the many and the need for perichoretic humility. *One* artist stands in relation to the *many* audience-members. An artwork stands in relation to many artworks. An audience-member stands in relation to many artworks. Each term can be applied to the others in what turns out to be a web of relationality. How to make sense of this web?

Artist Humility

An artist must deal with three things in any artistic endeavor: 1) The world and his materials which he must "re-create" (situation), 2) The rules of the art form he is working in (norms), 3) The personal feelings and ideas which motivate and sustain the work (existential). Readers may note that my scheme is derived from John Frame's perspectivalism.[5] Although Frame is dealing with theological and philosophical epistemology, I think his categories carry over into the arts. Since the artist is bound up with knowing the world, he faces the same philosophical problems as any knower. Insofar as he is also an active creator of "secondary meaning," as well as secondary worlds, it is imperative that we have a clear conception of the artistic process.

Again, complete specification is impossible, and even undesirable, but I believe that aesthetic confusion has resulted from not understanding how these proximate ends relate. The artist (one) is wrapped up within the world and his audience (many). How does the existential artist relate to the situational world, or to the norms of creation, tradition, or revelation? I don't pretend to fully answer these questions in this paper, but a step in the right direction would be to realize the importance of humility as an operational-principle. Artists do not have time to think through the deep, philosophical

---

5   See John Frame, *The Doctrine of the Knowledge of God* (Phillipsburg, NJ: P&R, 1987).

implications of everything they do, but they can create in a spirit of humility.

Artists should be primarily humble towards *God*, towards their *audience*, and toward their *work*. The artist must work within *norms*, within *community*, within his *own aesthetic sense*. There is danger of erring in any of these three areas.

The Artist & Humility Towards God and Men

The artist must be *theocentrically humble*. In Scripture nothing, least of all art, is autonomous. Everything must operate within God-ordained ends. Art serves God, by beautifying His house, either in the Old Covenant manifestations of the Tabernacle or Temple, or in the Earth that is his footstool. Artists themselves are given their artistic gifts by God.[6] Humility should characterize any endeavor where one serves and tries to please a superior. How much more humble should an artist be who is laboring to serve God? While contemporary artists are not in the same position as Bezalel and Aholiab, the makers of the tabernacle are still models for us. Just as Moses is an example in his great humility, so we should endeavor to emulate Old Covenant craftsmen in serving the Most High.

The Bible does not give us a complete aesthetic. There is no list of "thou shalts" and "shalt nots" for each of the arts. There are certain, broad commandments: not to make any idols, to think on what is true, honest, just, pure, and lovely, etc. (Phil. 4:8). We can also discover what God thought was beautiful in the specifications he gave for the building of his

---

[6] All good gifts, generally, are given by God (Jas. 1:17) and artistic skills, specifically, are given by God (Ex. 28:3).

houses. We can study Hebrew poetry, and note that the Levite-musicians were to play skillfully. We can know that God values balance, design, skillful craftsmanship, tension-and-rest, but there remains a great deal of latitude for the artist to explore and develop his gifts.

Maritain provides a wonderful picture of this freedom. He says that it would be futile to search for a single style or technique of Christian art, and that, "The art which germinates and grows in Christian man can admit of an infinity of them. But these forms will all have a family likeness, and all of them will differ substantially from non-Christian forms of art; as the flora of the mountains differs from the flora of the plains."[7] The great principle is that the artist should seek to glorify God in all his works. He should seek God's standards for beauty and excellence, and not impose his own aesthetic-of-the-month.

Devotion to God spills over in the works of our hands. Maritain stresses this need for theocentricity: "If the artist took the end of his art or the beauty of the work for the ultimate end of his operation and therefore for beatitude, he would be but an idolater. It is absolutely necessary therefore that the artist, *qua* man, work for something other than his work, for something better loved. God is infinitely more lovable than art."[8] The artist must work ultimately for God in order to avoid idolatry. But working for other proximate ends should restrain the artist from pride. The ends of the *work*, and the claims of the *audience* must also be considered.

Hence the artist must also be *homocentric*. He is part of the human race and needs to be in relation to others. The

---

7   Jacques Maritain, *Art and Scholasticism*, 68.

8   Maritain, *Art and Scholasticism*, 70.

autonomous artist, confident in his aesthetic superiority, cuts himself off from affirmation and from accountability. Annie Dillard notes that fiction,

> keeps its audience by retaining the world as its subject matter. People like the world. When the arts abandon the world as their subject matter, people abandon the arts. And when wide audiences abandon the arts, the arts are free to pursue whatever theories led them to abandon the world in the first place. They are as free as wandering albatrosses or stamp collectors or technical rock climbers; no one is looking.[9]

But artists should not be slavish in seeking audience response. They should care if no one is looking, but they should not go soliciting looks. There is the proverbial ditch on both sides of the road. Artists must not cow-tow to the audience, like Aaron fashioning the golden calf, but neither can they spurn their audience in a show of autonomy. The audience is not always right but nor is the artist. Following the Biblical injunction to consider others more highly than ourselves (Phil. 2:3) would go a long way in reducing so much of the name-calling that goes on in the art world.

The artist must be incorporated into the Christian community, and not left an island unto himself. He has been given gifts and talents which edify the body (Eph. 4:16). But he must also, in the act of joining a community, uphold the unity and laws of that community. There is such a thing as market pressures in art, and there is such a thing as bad art which the audience has a right to reject. Ideally, good art should be

---

[9] Annie Dillard, *Living By Fiction* (New York: Harper & Row), 79.

demanded by families, by the church, and by the state (in a limited sense).

The Artist & Humble Subjectivity

In writing about the painter James Whistler, G. K. Chesterton describes what we now think of as the quintessential artist: a somewhat eccentric, unpredictable man, with a lot of strange ideas that sometimes reach the heights of prophecy. But Chesterton argues that this type of artist is actually a bad artist, or at least a lesser artist. He writes:

> He [Whistler] was sometimes not even a great artist, because he thought so much about art. Any man with a vital knowledge of the human psychology ought to have the most profound suspicion of anybody who claims to be an artist, and talks a great deal about art. Art is a right and human thing, like walking or saying one's prayers; but the moment it begins to be talked about very solemnly, a man may be fairly certain that the thing has come into a congestion and a kind of difficulty...Artists of a large and wholesome vitality get rid of their art easily, as they breathe easily, or perspire easily. But in artists of less force, the thing becomes a pressure, and produces a definite pain, which is called the artistic temperament.[10]

The artist should strive to "breathe easily." More often than not, an artist is blessed with faculties of expression and feeling that others simply do not possess, but this does not give him the right to become a demi-god. His abilities do not give him

---

10 G. K. Chesterton, *Heretics* (New York: Devin-Adair, 1950), 243-244.

the right to pontificate or legislate. He is faced with a difficult task, like any serious and skillful worker. To whom much is given, much is required. The artist is called to be a master of both the Objective, and the Subjective. He is called to be a skillful craftsman, one who, in the writer Pierre Corneille's phrase, "loves the rules." In his Dedicatory Epistle to *La Suivante*, the French neo-classicist wrote: "'I love to follow the rules, but far from being their slave, I enlarge them or narrow them down according to the demands of my subject,' and even 'break without scruple' for the sake of beauty."[11] He loves the rules and breaks the rules in his pursuit of beauty and aesthetic value. He must *feel deeply*, and *work skillfully*.

The relation of these two proximate ends is a battleground where much artistic blood has been spilt. As we saw, the Romantics stressed the importance of emotions over rules, although they were still consummate craftsmen. Their experiment has come to an end, but self-expression is still the current absolute standard in modern art. Art must express something deep and personal, and preferably profound or philosophical.

There have been minor revolutions in modern art, however, that stress the importance of rules. Cubism, for instance, followed a rigid pattern even in its fragmentation. There are certain rules that guide the creation of a chaotic Cubist piece. In abstract art, there is the rule that nothing shall be represented. Certain twentieth-century artists, such as Picasso, Mondrian, Klee, and Beckmann, tended to be rather Platonic in their fascination with geometrical painting, and the forms of the world. Klee himself said: "What had already been

---

[11] Monroe Beardsley, *Aesthetics: From Classical Greece to the Present* (Tuscaloosa: University of Alabama, 1966), 145.

done for music by the end of the eighteenth century has at last been begun for the pictorial arts. Mathematics and physics furnished the means in the form of rules to be followed and to be broken."[12] These artists were not simply interested in self-expression. But, their philosophies were just as confused as pure self-expressionists because they had no ultimate ground for their rules.

The Christian artist seeks a balance, a synthesis of ends. This is, not surprisingly, the route the medievals took. According to Maritain, for the medievals, "...art was the science (*ars sine scientia nihil est*) of constructing objects according to their own laws. Art was not expression, but construction, an operation aiming at a certain result." He further shows that, "it is from the Renaissance with its superstitious reverence for antiquity and its stuffed Aristotle, not from the Christian Aristotle of our Doctors, that the starched rules of the grammarians of the *grand siecle* derive."[13] Like Corneille, the artist should love the rules, not only in following them, but in bending or twisting them as his artistic sense dictates: "[T]he artist is a ruler who uses rules according to his ends; it is as senseless to conceive of him as the slave of rules as to consider the worker the slave of his tools."[14]

An artist needs the humility appropriate to a ruler. He is a ruler in his art, but he is dependent on his subjects for his very life. No king exists in isolation. The artist is a ruler over his province, but he is also one subject among the subjects of a larger world. He is a ruler over his aesthetic emotions, and happily, these emotions are shared with most other people.

---

12 Klee in *Artists on Art*, 444.

13 Maritain, *Art and Scholasticism*, 38.

14 Maritain, *Art and Scholasticism*, 38.

The Christian artist should rejoice in *subjectivity*. By this, I do not mean "relativity," but am referring to the fact that man, as created beings, must receive all reality, all truth, from a higher being. Reality is mediated, and so is art. At its most basic level, art is a product of human eyes, of subjects.

As Rookmaaker put it, "art never copies nature, but always portrays reality in a human way."[15] Plato thought that art was thrice removed from the ultimate reality of the Forms, and was thus not trustworthy. He bequeathed a legacy of "representationality," which has haunted aesthetics until the present. The Christian artist need not worry too much about whether his art "represents" reality in some metaphysical sense. He is called simply to name the world appropriately, as a subject in submission to God.

The pagan artist must give meaning to his own work, but the Christian artist derives his meaning from God alone, and can then celebrate his own subjectivity. His feelings, his perceptions, his creations have meaning because they are reflections of God's creativity. Again, the formula boils down to *confidence and humility*. The artist should be a confident ruler, confident in his skills, yet humble in his administration of them. He is not the arbiter of taste. He does not generate the meaning for his autonomous works. He is subject to the market pressures of, hopefully, a well-educated audience. The web of relationality and proximate ends is once again unified through an attitude of humility. If we first seek the kingdom of God, all the rest will be given to us. Our task is not made any easier by seeking humility in the arts. Like the pursuit of any Good, it is infinitely harder in some respects. Marit-

---

15 H. R. Rookmaaker, *Modern Art and the Death of Culture* (Wheaton, IL: Crossway, 1970), 21.

ain, again: "Christianity does not make art easy. At the same time…it gives it what the artist has need of most—simplicity, the peace of awe and love, the innocence which renders matter docile to men and fraternal."[16]

Audience Humility

The humility that must be displayed in the nexus of relationality and proximate ends also helps us to understand the role of the audience. For most of human civilization art has been harnessed by the powers of the empires, rulers, and authoritarian states. There is no doubt that both artists and patrons have displayed unhealthy amounts of pride, particularly in the Renaissance. The Romantic and modern artist, with his newly discovered powers, pushed his autonomous authority to the limits. The result was his complete break with patronage in the eighteenth century. Then we find the image of the starving artist in his miserable garret. The artist now has a love-hate relationship with his patrons. He wants their support, indeed cannot live without it, but still resents it highly. He is thrilled when they buy his work for $100,000, but when they laugh at it, he derides them as uncultured swine!

Thomas Craven, formerly one of America's foremost art critics, contrasted the modern situation with the Greek: "The esthetic Hellens needed sculptures—as my own son needs music and sports—and were equipped to make stern appraisals of the efforts of artists, and to compel them to do their level best or be sent to barbarian lands in disgrace. Today there is no intelligent check on the propensities of the artist,

---

16 Maritain, *Art and Scholasticism*, 69.

and wildest, and frequently idiotic, propensities are exploited by critics and magazine editors out to capitalize on anything sensational."[17] The artist vaunts his autonomy in the face of his patrons and in the face of the art world.

C. S. Lewis, in *Surprised By Joy*, supplies a perfect picture of audience humility:

> I was in the midst of the Romantics now. There was a humility in me (as a reader) at that time which I shall never recapture. Some poems I could not enjoy as well as others. It never occurred to me that these might be the inferior ones; I merely thought that I was getting tired of my author or was not in the right mood.[18]

Lewis is certainly describing an extreme form of audience humility at an early stage of his career as a literary connoisseur. However, it would be better to pass through this naïve stage of humility than tromp through the Western canon with a prideful air of knowing-it-all.

There is something to be learned from every author, even if a certain author teaches us what to avoid, or is a perfect example of atrocious art. The proper attitude toward a work of art is first *reception*, then *questioning/ understanding*, and finally *judgment*. This is a similar scheme to that outlined in Mortimer J. Adler's *How to Read a Book*, and seems to follow the natural progression of human knowledge. How can we judge a thing if we do not first understand it? How can we understand a thing if we do not ask questions of it, and how can we ask questions if we do not receive it?

---

17 Thomas Craven, *The Pocket Book of Greek Art* (New York: Pocket Books, Inc., 1950), 67.

18 C. S. Lewis, *Surprised By Joy* (San Diego: Harcourt Brace & Co., 1955),163.

We may decide after all that Schoenberg was out to lunch. But can we really say that if we do not understand him? Can we condemn Picasso simply because we can't quite see what's lurking in the cubist painting? I think there are strong reasons for speaking very strongly against these artists, but I hope no one would give my opinion a second thought unless I displayed a good grasp of what Schoenberg and Picasso were trying to do in their art.

For the Christian, the issue of audience humility is even sharper. We must provide answers to the dying hopes of the autonomous art world. Rookmaaker drives the point home as he writes: "This art is the work of your neighbours, your contemporaries, human beings who are crying out in despair for the loss of their humanity, their values, their lost absolutes, groping in the dark for answers. It is already late, if not too late, but if we want to help our generation we must hear their cry. We must listen to them as they cry out from their prison, the prison of a universe which is aimless, meaningless, absurd."[19]

Although many of the uncultured swine *are* simply uncultured swine, much art world rhetoric is an elitist reaction to these Philistines. We form our separate clubs and draw up manifestos, ignoring the commandments to be of one mind. But both the artist and the audience are simultaneously in the dual roles of *teacher* and *student*. Both have valid concerns, and can learn from the other. This is not simply a plea for "dialogue" or getting along nicely. There is good and bad art, but neither party has the authority to legislate absolutely. I believe that only humility can provide a framework for balancing these dual roles and the claims of relationality.

---

19 H. R. Rookmaaker, *Modern Art*, 136.

Humility & the Question of Canon

The perichoretic balance that we must humbly seek in the art world corresponds to the issue of creedal authority in the Church. More specifically, honoring/deferring to the canon is much the same as honoring the Creeds/ Fathers. I do not believe that the Romanist doctrine of the magisterium is Biblical, but I do believe that the Church is the pillar and ground of the church (1 Tim. 3:15), against which the gates of Hades shall not prevail (Mt. 16:18). Creeds have real authority, insofar as they accurately reflect and summarize the doctrines of Scripture. The Fathers of the Church also deserve our respect and study, simply because they are our fathers in the faith. They came before us, and faced many of the same problems in different guises. Only a foolish son rejects the wisdom of his elders, and only the ignorant pride of the modern evangelical refuses to even consider what the Fathers have said.

In artistic matters, there is no promise given, but there is still a received body of works that are almost universally esteemed as worthy of praise and study. Clement Greenberg, arguably the most important art critic of the latter half of the twentieth century has said: "Taste has varied, but not beyond certain limits...We may have come to prefer Giotto to Raphael, but we still do not deny that Raphael was one of the best painters of his time. There has been an agreement then, and this agreement rests, I believe, on a fairly constant distinction made between those values only to be found in art and the values which can be found elsewhere."[20] He also

---

20 Clement Greenberg, *Art and Culture* (Boston, MA: Beacon Press, 1961), 13.

asserted that, "Major art is impossible, or almost so, without a thorough assimilation of the major art of the preceding period or periods."[21]

The ancient masters should not be slavishly imitated, except perhaps in the earliest stages of artistic development, but they should be studied. We are given the opportunity to stand on the shoulders of giants (another favorite concept of the medievals), and we would either be prideful or foolish to reject it. The neoclassical giant Ingres concurred: "Our task is not to invent but to continue, and we have enough to do if, following the examples of the masters, we utilize those innumerable types which nature constantly offers to us, if we interpret them with wholehearted sincerity and ennoble them through that pure and firm style without which no work has beauty."[22]

Arthur Versluis expresses similar sentiments when he addresses the issue of the canon: "For the essence of any traditional canon is the subordination of the artist to that which he is trying to convey or transmit. To one who arrogantly insists upon his 'originality,' the test of art is its divergence from the past, an attitude that produces the banality of virtually all contemporary art; but the traditional artist sees himself as a vehicle for greatness that far exceeds his own capacity or significance."[23] A humble view of the artist sees him as part of a greater whole. He finds himself in the midst of a great river, which is carrying him forward quite against his will. The test of a great artist is how well he assimilates the glories of the

---

21 Greenberg, *Art and Culture*, 210.

22 Jean Auguste Dominique Ingres, *Artists On Art*, 216.

23 Arthur Versluis in David W. Hall, *The Arrogance of the Modern: Historical Theology Held in Contempt* (Powder Springs, GA: The Covenant Foundation, 1997), 27.

past, as well as developing his own gifts, and the inevitable perspective that he has as a man of his own time.[24] Hopefully his own period will not fade away into a minor eddy in the ever-flowing river.

T. S. Eliot brilliantly summarizes the situation of the artist in relation to the past in his essay, "Tradition and the Individual Talent." He asserts that the artist is not autonomous: "No poet, no artist of any art, has his complete meaning alone...You cannot value him alone; you must set him, for contrast and comparison, among the dead."[25] This historical sense is what gives an artist his place, as well as giving the audience a context for appreciating and judging his accomplishments. Far from limiting the artist, a historical sense gives him form and freedom: "This historical sense, which is a sense of the timeless as well as of the temporal and of the timeless and of the temporal together, is what makes a writer traditional. And it is at the same time what makes a writer most acutely conscious of his place in time, of his contemporaneity."[26] Again, this is the paradox of humility. If we lose ourselves in the canon, we find ourselves, and find a greater originality.

The nature of the artist's relation to the canon is best illustrated by the paradoxical nature of injunctions to humility (Phil. 2:3), and the reality of generational progression. David is able to say, "I have more understanding than all my teachers: for thy testimonies are my meditation. I understand more

---

[24] Cf. Borges, who, among modern writers, has a profound awareness of the paradoxes of time: "To be modern is to be contemporary, of our own time; inevitably, we must be so," in Jorge Luis Borges, *Selected Poems*, 35.

[25] Frank Kermode, ed., *Selected Prose of T. S. Eliot* (San Diego: Harcourt, Inc., 1975), 38.

[26] *Selected Prose of T. S. Eliot*, 38.

than the ancients, because I keep thy precepts" (Ps. 119:99–100). David is undoubtedly far superior than his fathers in the faith, but he goes forward by thoroughly assimilating the religious canon of Israel. Of course, he understands more than the ancients because he endeavors to understand the most important things first. No doubt the incomparable poetry that flowed from David's hands was only possible because of his devotion to God. Artists should learn from his example.

The inviolable law of the universe is, "before honor is humility" (Prov. 15:33; 18:12). The artist must seek to be instructed humbly in the art of the past, as well as in the "fear of the Lord," which is the "instruction of wisdom" (Prov. 15:33). An artist who studies the canon is in a place to surpass the wisdom of the ancients. The artist studied in the wisdom of God is given access to the treasures of the universe.

It is only humility that can give us the proper attitude toward the canon, and this applies to both audience and artist. The *audience* needs to be educated in both theological and aesthetic matters. My personal taste may not be in accord with Scripture, or may be dictated by the revolutionary fervor of the present art-establishment. I will only become aware of my anachronistic taste if I immerse myself in the great works (and some of the trivial) of the past. The *artist* needs to develop his gifts in order to glorify God, and if, after immersion in the canon, he is not painting like Da Vinci, he will either have a good reason not to, or will start wondering what's wrong with himself. A perichoretic humility acknowledges the importance of both artist and audience in the community of the art world.

Artwork Humility

T. S. Eliot was an undisputed master of the Western Canon. Yet paradoxically, his mastery of the canon made him unique, and his work has changed the face of modern poetry. He denied strenuously that the artist exists autonomously or is self-sufficient. Not only did he maintain that an individual artist stands in relation to the canon, but he thought of individual art-works as existing in relation to each other. He described this relation as constituting an "ideal order:"

> The existing monuments form an ideal order among themselves, which is modified by the introduction of the new (the really new) work of art among them. The existing order is complete before the new work arrives; for order to persist after the supervention of novelty, the whole existing order must be, if ever so slightly, altered; and so the relations, proportions, values of each work of art toward the whole are readjusted; and this is conformity between the old and the new.[27]

Of course, this order is always perceived and mediated by human beings in relation to the art-works. The ideal order does not exist autonomously. However, there is a real sense in which the creation of any new artwork changes our perceptions of the canon. Eliot's conception is useful in that it helps us to appreciate the fundamental relationality that characterizes art, as well as every human endeavor.

Art is ontologically dependent. It is firstly dependent on God, then on created materials (in music, on sound waves),

---

27 *Selected Prose of T. S. Eliot*, 38.

and finally on human perception. Hence Michelangelo's *David* cannot vaunt itself against all authority, assuming it carries such humanistic meaning as is commonly attributed to it. The best work of an artist is dependent on a multitude of factors for its greatness. The artwork cannot feel humility in response to its own dependency, but a human observer should understand this. This realization should make us more responsible viewers of art, and not abject worshipers.

But the fact that art cannot be actively humble or prideful does not prevent us from seeing either pride or humility expressed in an artwork. An artist may be prideful, and in creating, he makes his work prideful. The metaphysical pride of the cubists is manifested in their painting. Their work manifests a metaphysical conceit by which they think they have a right to break God's world into pieces. Unless ontologically humble, painting becomes infatuated with itself, degenerating into a cubist surface. As Greenberg observed, painting finally becomes about painting. The autonomous artist is expressing himself accurately, and creates a self-referencing work. But because he cannot give his own meaning to either himself or his work, his work ultimately tends towards absurdity. In this way, the artwork itself can be a vehicle for pride and autonomy.

There is a sense in which art is only concerned with itself, as Aquinas and Maritain hold.[28] Art can only be concerned with making a good artwork. Artistic knowledge and skill may have parallels in other areas of life, but it has no dominion over them, as those maintain who make their life

---

28 Jacques Maritain writes: "[I]n the production of the work the virtue of art aims only at one thing: the good of the work-to-be-made, beauty to be made to shine in matter, the creating of the thing according to its own laws, independently of all the rest," *Essay on Art* (New York: Charles Scribner's Sons), 89.

revolve around art. Maritain maintains that art must be ruled by the higher virtue of prudence and this can certainly be expanded to include all of God's revealed world.

Unless the artwork (while still concerned only for its own good) is brought into humble submission to God, it becomes an idol that claims the very life of man. This is the point of the ghost in *The Great Divorce*: "It was all a snare. Ink and catgut and paint were necessary down there, but they are also dangerous stimulants. Every poet and musician and artist, but for Grace, is drawn away from love of the thing he tells, to the love of telling till, down in Deep Hell, they cannot be interested in God at all but only in what they say about Him. For it doesn't stop at being interested in paint, you know. They sink lower—become interested in their own personalities and then in nothing but their own reputations."[29]

Charles Baudelaire, no stranger to fierce passion, describes the same process, which is really that of artistic idolatry: "Absorbed…by the fierce passion for the beautiful, the droll, the pretty, the picturesque…the notion of what is proper and true disappear. The frenzied passion for art is a cancer which eats up everything else."[30] By remaining humble, and not attributing false powers to his art, the artist will avoid artistic idolatry, and be freed to pursue his art truly. Again, the focus is primarily on the artist (although art has a life of its own, as every writer and artist will testify). Unless art is governed by higher ends, by theo/ homocentricity, it becomes its own end, swallowing up the artist in its autonomy.

A humble attitude towards the arts in relation (and particular artworks in relation) will heighten appreciation of all

---

29 C. S. Lewis, *The Great Divorce* (New York: Touchstone, 1946), 80.

30 Charles Baudelaire in Jacques Maritain, *An Essay in Art*, 90.

types of art. There is truth, goodness, and beauty in the most simple, or primitive of forms, as well as in the most complex and profound. As Borges wrote: "The steely music of the Saxon language is no less agreeable than the delicate musings of the Symbolists. Each subject, however occasional or thin, imposes on us its own aesthetic."[31] An artist who has a humble view toward his work will shun the manifesto-writing revolutionaries who think their own forms are bringing the new heavens and new earth.

A humble artist accepts the *limitations of his medium*. In an essay on Cézanne, Greenberg describes the famous artist as always trying to overcome, or go beyond, the limits of his canvas in his depth-experiments.[32] The experiment was doomed to failure, simply because an artist cannot escape the limits of the world. It seems Cézanne could not accept these limits: "he complained till his last day of his inability to 'realize'…Every brush-stroke that followed a fictive plane into fictive depth harked back—by reason of its abiding, unequivocal character as a mark made by a brush—to the physical fact of the medium."[33]

The humble artist does not need to fight his materials (except in the futility that oppresses all of fallen creation). As Chesterton put it in his inimitable way: "The artist loves his limitations: they constitute the thing he is doing. The painter is glad that the canvas is flat. The sculptor is glad that the clay is colourless."[34] While embracing these limitations, the artist must submit to the good of his work. The balance,

---

31 Borges, *Selected Poems*, 371.

32 Greenberg, *Art and Culture*, 55.

33 Greenberg, *Art and Culture*, 55.

34 G. K. Chesterton, *Orthodoxy* (New York: John Lane Company, 1908), 72.

proportion, and consonance that makes art good is not arbitrarily imposed on his materials. In order to achieve aesthetic effects, the artist must use God-ordained means. By creating a symbolic humility in his work (each element humbly in relation to the other: color to color, tone to tone, scene to plot, etc.), the artist creates good art. In this the artist is both limited by, and the ruler of, aesthetic effects. An artist should be humble in relation to his materials. He must give himself, totally, to his art, humbly, seeking to understand the strengths and weaknesses of his medium. Then, after years of toil, he may expect to reap the reward. Before honor is humility. Eliot calls the process a self-sacrifice, "What happens is a continual surrender of himself as he is at the moment to something which is more valuable. The progress of an artist is a continual self-sacrifice, a continual extinction of personality."[35] The artist should serve his art with the humility of a ruler, like Christ. He must lose himself in his art, only to find himself again. In humble submission to the rules and requirements of his work, he may receive the honor of having others say to his artwork, "It is good."

---

35 *Selected Prose of T. S. Eliot*, 40

Conclusion

> Behold how green this valley is; also how beautiful with lilies. I have also known many labouring that have got good estates in this Valley of Humiliation; for God resisteth the proud, but gives more, more grace to the humble. For indeed it is a very fruitful soil, and doth bring forth by handfuls.
>
> - John Bunyan, *Pilgrim's Progress*

> Take not thy thunder from us,
> But take away our pride.
>
> - G. K. Chesterton, *A Hymn*

Tossing "humility" into the philosophy of aesthetics may seem like a cop-out. How foolish to be obsessing about a dated theological concept, when we could be talking about *A Quasi-Survey of Some "Minimalist" Tendencies in the Quantitatively Minimal Dance Activity Midst the Plethora*, or *Art As Internal Technology: The Return of the Shaman—The Descent of the Goddess?*[36] Well, God has used foolishness before, and quite effectively for that matter:

> But God hath chosen the foolish things of the world to confound the wise; and God hath chosen the weak things of the world to confound the things that are mighty; And base things of the world, and things which are despised, hath God chosen, yea, and things which are not, to bring

---

[36] I didn't make these titles up. The inquisitive reader can read the essays in *Esthetics Contemporary*, ed. Richard Kostelanetz (Buffalo, NY: Prometheus Books, 1978).

to nought things that are: That no flesh should glory in his presence (1 Cor. 1:27–29, KJV).

God has chosen the laughter of a child to confound the pronouncements of the artistic elite. He has chosen the scribblings of a retarded adult to confound Picasso. The heavens and earth cannot contain the glory of the Lord, but yet he chose Solomon, with all his tragic flaws, to build him a measly little house (1 Kgs 8:27). Mt. Sinai trembles and burns at his presence, but he condescends to give Bezalel and Aholiab artistic skill and knowledge (Ex. 35:31).

Only humble devotion to God will save us from artistic idolatry. All the aesthetic wonders of the world will eventually fade away. We would do well to remember the words of Michelangelo when he said, "'Neither painting nor sculpture,' said Michelangelo in his old age, 'will any longer charm the soul that is turned towards that divine love which opens out its arms on the Cross to receive us.'"[37]

In proposing an aesthetics of humility, we must also avoid the "manifesto syndrome." We don't want to be like the ghost of an artist in *The Great Divorce*, running away from the brink of heavenly bliss to start a "movement:" "'I must be off at once,'" said the Ghost. 'Let me go! Damn it all, one has one's duty to the future of Art. I must go back to my friends. I must write an article. There must be a manifesto. We must start a periodical. We must have publicity. Let me go. This is beyond a joke!'"[38] It is always a temptation to seize upon some theological doctrine, and use it as the magic key to unlock all aesthetic, ethical, or cultural questions. However, I do think

---

37 Maritain, *Art and Scholasticism*, 80–81.

38 Lewis, *The Great Divorce*, 82.

that aesthetic humility is foundational. It requires humility to even have a correct view of other doctrines. The mind must submit itself in faith. Then it can proceed in humility. God uses humbling to teach his people important lessons:

> And he humbled thee, and suffered thee to hunger, and fed thee with manna, which thou knewest now, neither did thy fathers know; that he might make thee know that man doth not live by bread only, but by every word that proceedeth out of the mouth of the Lord doth man live (Deut. 8:3).

> Who fed thee in the wilderness with manna, which thy fathers knew not, that he might humble thee, and that he might prove thee, to do thee good at thy latter end (Deut. 8:16).

We have been led into an artistic wilderness. As Rookmaaker wrote, "We have lost so much in our civilization (and we Christians are also responsible for the fact) that the way will be long and tiring. But perhaps we can lay a foundation for the next generation."[39] We will not be producing works to rival the medieval cathedrals, or the Dutch masters within our own lifetimes. Our task is not to produce a vibrant, beautiful civilization by our own genius and hard work. We hardly know what such a culture would look like. All we can do is humbly submit to God's norms for our lives, and for our culture. Perhaps when our children and children's children have been raised in a more beautiful world, they may take up the task which we were too weak to perform. But, they too will

---

39 Rookmaaker, *Modern Art*, 245.

be helpless unless God is merciful and pours his Spirit out upon them.

If God is merciful to us, we cannot forget what Moses told the people not to say, "My power and the might of mine hand hath gotten this wealth" (Deut. 8:17). We must build in an attitude of Solomonic humility. Borges wrote: "Nothing is built on stone, everything on sand, but our duty is to build as if sand were stone."[40] We are to build in humility. The rest is up to God. *The good artist must work for eternity, so far as the fragility of things human allows it*: Sebastiano Conca.[41]

We can only pray we will learn the lesson of the Israelites. God has given us over to futility for a time, but if He should grant us artistic reformation, we must abhor any pride in our beautiful poems, our stunning paintings, our sublime music. It is only ours because it was given to us by God. To Him be all the thanks, and all the glory.

☐

Dr. Gregory Soderberg (PhD VU-Amsterdam) is a Lead Teacher for Logos Online School, a Teaching Fellow at the BibleMesh Institute, and a Mentor-Professor for Redemption Seminary. He is the author of *As Often As You Eat This Bread: Communion Frequency in English, Scottish, and Early American Churches* (V&R), and has contributed chapters to three other books. He has written for *Intellectual Takeout* and blogs at The SoderBlog.

---

40 Borges, *Selected Poems*, 295.

41 Robert Goldwater and Marco Treves, eds., "Artists on Art," Internet Archive, January 1, 1970, https://archive.org/details/artistsonart0000unse_a7z0/mode/2up, 163.

Review of *In the Beauty of Holiness* by David Lyle Jeffrey

by Robert M. Woods, PhD

Jeffrey, David Lyle. *In the Beauty of Holiness: Art and the Bible in Western Culture.* Grand Rapids, Michigan: William B. Eerdmans Publishing Company, 2017, hardcover, $49.00, 448 pp.

The eminent Sociologist of Culture, Philip Rieff, in his *My Life Among the Deathworks: Illustrations of the Aesthetics of Authority* explored and explicated what he classified as key deathworks. In his analysis, Rieff chronicled the shifting ways of apprehending all intimations of the spiritually embodied social thought and artifacts. He persuasively argued that the modern world is a "third" type of culture in western history. It is this third, death-loving culture that waged all out war on all preceding cultural authority with the ultimate goal of creating a culture/non-culture empty of any hint of the holy and bereft of beauty as traditionally understood.

Dr. David Lyle Jeffrey of Baylor University has authored a marvelous and truly beautiful book that explores the interplay of the Bible and art. The reader can readily imagine this book as the antidote to the toxic death culture. Simply put, this important work is an engagement and celebration of life works of the past two thousand years. Jeffrey frames his presentation in terms of a story—beginning with the catacombs, rich with imagery, to select modern examples. Story is an interpretive lens as the select examples both illustrate Biblical truths and also serve as works of interpretation. In other words, visual images offer interpretations or stand as a hermeneutical action.

Dr. Jeffrey's lovely book, *In the Beauty of Holiness*, embodies more than four decades of reverent scholarship. Jeffrey affirms that this book is "not a history of art, even of Christian art in the European tradition," but is designed to shed light on a narrower theme which is the, "trajectory for Christian art in the west." In this book, Jeffrey engages well-known artists that portray Biblical scenes. There are a number of Biblical moments that are recurring and popular among visual artists. The birth narrative, and Jesus's baptism and passion are subjects rich with details easily translated to visual images. Some attention is also given to the types and motivations for both artists and patrons.

A particularly strong chapter addresses select works of art that stand in opposition to the story Jeffrey unfolds. In the chapter "Art Against Belief," Jeffrey hones in on some works by Salvador Dali and Pablo Picasso. Despite the practice that these artists used religious imagery, their engagement was mainly in defiance or dissent from traditional Christianity. Jeffrey does conclude this section with some attention to works that are more complimentary of the consensus in handling the faith expressed in artistic forms.

Although Dr. Jeffrey's research is primarily on the interplay between the Christian story on the visual arts, as an interdisciplinary Humanist, he often brings music and poetry into the conversation. One minor point of objection that some Cultural Historians may dissent from Dr. Jeffrey is how he places the blame for a shift or discontinuity from the early Church and later Baroque and Enlightenment artists within the Renaissance (specifically) and not within the Reformation. Jeffrey notes, "Until the Renaissance beauty and holiness were intimately conjoined in art for worship, evoking the presence of the holy for believers"[1] but this cohesive vision was later fragmented by a new engagement with the arts more generally characterized by crass acquisition. Also, by "the late medieval to the early modern period...biblical subjects and narratives, especially stories with erotic potential...became occasions for an indulgence in beauty 'for beauty's sake...'" signaling "the commodification of sexual beauty and voyeurism."[2] Of the many sub-themes Dr. Jeffrey examines, one that has occupied considerable attention in the history of the Christian faith is the human body, specifically the nude human figure. Nudity, depending on how portrayed, can communicate natural, virtuous, and even spiritual truths. This range of ways nudity is captured varies depending on era, artist, and subject matter.

The book is divided into two main sections with twelve chapters. In the first half, Jeffrey describes a grand synthesis. Dr. Jeffrey begins with a careful exploration of the way that Sacred Scripture demonstrates the essential relationship between holiness and that which is beautiful. Jeffrey masterfully interacts with a wide range of artistic images, architecture,

---

[1] David Lyle Jeffrey, *In the Beauty of Holiness: Art and the Bible in Western Culture* (Grand Rapids, MI: William B. Eerdmans Publishing Company), 5.

[2] Jeffrey, *In the Beauty of Holiness*, 6.

and liturgy to generously show the harmonious union in faith and practice.

In the second part of *In the Beauty of Holiness*, the story turns toward the direction of the modern and later post-modern disconnect between faith and art. Early the disintegration is located within the schematic Christendom, and later found among religious dissenters. Jeffrey even examines select artists who use Christian signs and symbols primarily to attack. Specifically in chapters, titled "Art after Belief" and "Art against Belief," Dr. Jeffrey tracks the ways in which nature replaced the Christian faith as found in Romanticism, but then later how art became a surrogate religion with artists such as Gauguin and the Pre-Raphaelites. It is in the chapter that examines select works by Pablo Picasso and Salvador Dali to demonstrate how even these artists "used" religious imagery to show specific religious dissent.

It is fitting to read Dr. Jeffrey's book as a visual theology seeking the good, the truth, and the holy Being. As a visual engagement of the beauty of holiness, it is a unique work. One could imagine that due to the wide historical scope of this volume, generalists will receive greater pleasure than specialists who may note "all that is missing" or the "lack of depth." Despite the limitations of any single volume spanning two thousand years and such a vast subject (beauty in art), in less than four hundred pages Jeffrey provides a feast for the eyes, mind, and soul.

Dr. Jeffrey does not shy away from counter-cultural scholarship by modeling clear and consistent Christian thinking. Part of that counter-cultural tendency is seen with an insistence of a master narrative. Much of the benefit of this book rests with Jeffrey's skill at both analytical and synthetic engagement with primary and secondary sources. Jeffrey does not and should not ignore a traditional notion of the humanities as a unified grand narrative in the West fully informed by Christian conviction. From a scholarly and human perspective, there is much in this book to delight the eyes and the mind. It is so encouraging to encounter this level of scholarship practiced within the boundaries of a robust orthodox Christian faith.

This beautifully illustrated and soundly explicated book would be the perfect book for an Art survey class or general Humanities course within Classical Christian schools and Christian colleges/universities and would most certainly edify any teacher or student who has been educated in art and architecture, philosophy, theology, biblical studies, liturgy, aesthetics and other humane subjects.

In the epilogue, Jeffrey writes of his intentions with this book: "As we have seen, the annals of Western art bear witness to the perserverant power of biblical narrative to engage the heart, especially by artists whose imaginations have been continuously reformed both by the legacy of earlier Christian art and by reading the Bible."[3] Woven throughout this book is the truth that beauty, while ephemeral and fleeting, can be redeemed within the cosmic picture. The Bible speaks of the eternal nature of the good, true, and holy beautiful. It is in this related sense that similar to prayer that is also ephemeral and fleeting, is intertwined with the immortal.

---

3   Jeffrey, *In the Beauty of Holiness*, 364.

Robert M. Woods is Headmaster of Veritas Christian Academy, A Classical Christian School in Fletcher, NC and a Teaching Fellow for Faulkner University's MA/PhD programs in the Humanities.

The Question of the Nude

Guidance for Classical Christian Educators

by Joshua Herring, MA

In *My Name is Asher Lev*, Chaim Potok evokes tension between the protagonist's Hasidic identity and his artistic development. Asher faces a crucible-type moment when he discovers the nude; his teacher explains that Asher will

> see more crucifixions and more nativities and more Greek and Roman gods and more scenes of war and love—because that is the world of art, Asher Lev. And we will see more naked women, and you will learn the reason for the differences between the naked women of Titian and those of Rubens. This is the world you want to make sacred. You had better learn it well first before you begin.[1]

The painting of nudes violates strong *mores* of Asher's Hasidim, but represents a tool he must acquire if he will enter the world of *goyishe* art. In using this plot device, Potok illustrates the central place the nude holds within fine art. His analysis is supported by the agreement of art history, literature, and

---

1 Chaim Potok, *My Name is Asher Lev* (New York: Anchor Books, 2000), 228.

museums worldwide: the tradition of painting and sculpting nude human forms is as old as human civilization. Aestheticians, art critics, and philosophers have commented over the centuries on the meaning of the nude in art; while most voices agree that the nude is a significant element of visual vocabulary, the meaning of that vocabulary is subject to debate.

Across the last three centuries, different authors have found varying meanings in the artistic nude. Through surveying representative voices in aesthetics, and exploring two opposed theories of art, the need for a different answer to the question of nude emerges. By grounding the nude in a philosophical anthropology constructed through insights from Gadamer and Christian theology, this art form receives a foundation particularly helpful to those in the classical renewal movement.

I. An Aesthetic Survey

In his *Introductory Lectures on Aesthetics*, Hegel tasks fine art with enlivening and bringing into materiality the Idea:

> [...] art is what cheers and animates the dull and withered dryness of the idea, reconciles with reality its abstractions and dissociation therefrom, and supplies out of the real world what is lacking from the notion, it follows, we may think, that a *purely* intellectual treatment of art destroys this very means of supplementation, annihilates it, and reduces the idea once more to its simplicity devoid of reality, and to its shadowy abstractness.[2]

---

2 G. W. F. Hegel, *Introductory Letters on Aesthetics*, trans. Bernard Bosanquet (New York: Penguin Classics, 2004), 8.

Fine art moves the Idea from spiritual to material existence, and in so doing both the Idea and the work of art increase in meaning. Hegel argues that "[...] the content of art is the Idea, and that its form lies in the plastic use of images accessible to sense."[3] In order to make the Idea sensible, the artist selects the form proper to the Idea he seeks to convey. Such a form, Hegel suggests, must meet certain criteria:

> If a true and therefore concrete content is to have corresponding to it a sensuous form and modelling, this sensuous form must [...] be no less emphatically something individual, wholly concrete in itself, and one. [...] The natural shape of the human body is such a sensuous concrete as is capable of representing spirit, which is concrete in itself, and of displaying itself in conformity therewith.[4]

The unity Hegel requires for the expression of the Idea is found in the "natural shape" of the human forms. In a view derived from the doctrine of the *imago dei*, Hegel presents the human form as bridging the spiritual and physical: "This shape, with which the Idea as Spiritual—as individually determinate spirituality—invests itself when manifested as a temporal phenomenon, is the *human form*."[5] The nude becomes a way of depicting that which cannot take physical form. In fine art, the nude communicates ideas in an understandable form.

Leo Tolstoy in *What is Art?* opposes the use of nudes in art. His opening question applies not just to the sacrifices made by the archetypal starving artist, but also to questions of morality and modesty: "It is said that this is done for the

---

3   Hegel, *Introductory Letters on Aesthetics*, 76.

4   Hegel, *Introductory Letters on Aesthetics*, 77.

5   Hegel, *Introductory Letters on Aesthetics*, 86.

sake of art, and that art is a very important thing. But is it true that this is art, and that art is such an important thing that such sacrifices should be offered to it?"[6] Modern art by Tolstoy's time had replaced a unifying vision, the task of older artists, with objects of lust. "Later the element of sexual lust began to enter art more and more, becoming (with very few exceptions, and in novels and dramas no exceptions) the necessary condition of every work of art of the wealthy classes."[7] Where other critics saw beauty and technical skill, Tolstoy understood the nude as an upper-class method of stimulating erotic desire.

> The majority of paintings by French artists portray female nakedness in various forms. There is hardly a page or poem in the new French literature without a description of nakedness or the use here and there, appropriately or inappropriately, of the favorite word and notion *nu* ['nude']. [...] the entire artistic world of Europe and America imitates these people suffering from erotic mania.[8]

The reduction of the nude to decoration symbolized the degradation of art in the rise of the mass-production economy. In such a world, Tolstoy argues,

> any reasonable and moral person would again decide the question the way it was decided by Plato for his republic and by all Church Christian and Mohammedan teachers of mankind—that is, he would say, "Better that there be no

---

6 Leo Tolstoy, *What is Art?*, trans. Richard Pevear and Larissa Volokhonsky (New York: Penguin Books, 1995), 8.

7 Tolstoy, *What is Art?*, 61.

8 Tolstoy, *What is Art?*, 62–63.

art than that the depraved art, or a simulacrum of it, which exists now should continue."[9]

Before one can improve the condition of modern art, Tolstoy argues, one must first recognize the problem: "The art of our time and circle has become a harlot. [...] This the people of our time and circle must understand in order to get rid of the filthy stream of this depraved, lascivious art that is drowning us."[10] The use of the nude in art represented not the triumph of the human imagination but its baseness; the nude stimulated lust, and the highest forms of art were nothing but glorified pornography.

In contrast to Tolstoy, Roger Scruton links the nude to the communication of the soul as embodied.

> A body is an assemblage of body parts; an embodied person is a free being revealed in the flesh. When we speak of a beautiful human body we are referring to the beautiful embodiment of a person, and not to a body considered merely as such.[11]

The extent to which the viewer can perceive the soul in the face of the person is the measure of the artist's success. While the face is the most evident way of communicating the soul, Scruton includes the whole body in this act of communication:

> The distinctive beauty of the human body derives from its nature as an embodiment. Its beauty is not the beauty of

---

9   Tolstoy, *What is Art?*, 146.

10 Tolstoy, *What is Art?*, 150.

11 Roger Scruton, *Beauty: A Very Short Introduction* (Oxford: Oxford University Press, 2011), 40.

a doll, and is something more than a matter of shape and proportion. When we find human beauty represented in a statue, such as the *Apollo Belvedere* or the *Daphne of Bernini*, what is represented is the beauty of a person—flesh animated by the individual soul, and expressing individuality in all its parts.[12]

Scruton suggests that there is a special place for considering the way in which the face allows the viewer to see not just the work of art, but the person depicted. He writes,

> Whether it attracts contemplation or prompts desire, human beauty is seen in personal terms. It resides especially in those features—the face, the eyes, the lips, and hands—through which we relate to each other I to I. Although there may be fashions in human beauty, and although different cultures may embellish the body in different ways, the eyes, the mouth and hands have a universal appeal. For they are the features from which the soul of another person shines on us, and makes itself known.[13]

The nude becomes a place for the artist to reveal the soul to the viewer as an embodied person; the soul of the subject reveals itself through the body.

Hegel and Scruton agree in arguing for the material representation of the immaterial through bodily forms, while Tolstoy stands aghast at the presence of nudity in fine art, rejecting the artistic theory of ideas communicated through nude forms. The nude remains a significant source of artistic creation and technical skill, and in the past seventy years two primary theories account for this reality among art critics.

---

[12] Roger Scruton, *Beauty*, 41.

[13] Scruton, *Beauty*, 41.

II. Traditional Formalist vs. Progressive Psychoanalytic Approaches to the Nude

Sir Kenneth Clark wrote the definitive study on the nude's meaning, evolution, and value in western culture.[14] Clark develops a particular theory of the nude, tracing that theory across ancient, medieval, Renaissance, modern, and (for his 1950s time period) contemporary works. His theory of the nude is the one later scholars build on, disagree with, and interact with to construct their own approaches. Clark explains that the nude is "an art form invented by the Greeks in the fifth century..." intended to display an ideal rather than strict representation.[15] That ideal shifts across time, culture, and artist, but, Clark contends, the nude is always idealized. He contrasts the artistic nude with the photograph of a naked person:

> [...] the result [of a photograph] is hardly ever satisfactory to those whose eyes have grown accustomed to the harmonious simplifications of antiquity. We are immediately disturbed by wrinkles, pouches, and other small imperfections, which, in the classical scheme, are eliminated. By long habit we do not judge it as a living organism, but as a design; and we discover that the transitions are inconclusive, the outline is faltering. We are bothered because the various parts of the body cannot be perceived as simple units and have no clear relationship to one another. In al-

---

14 Richard Leppert, *The Nude: The Cultural Rhetoric of the Body in the Art of Western Modernity* (Boulder, CO: Westview Books, 2007), 8.

15 Kenneth Clark, *The Nude: A Study in Ideal Form* (Princeton, NJ: Princeton University Press, 1972), 4

most every detail the body is not the shape that art had led us to believe it should be.[16]

The nude smooths out the realities of individual bodies. The goal is not realistic representation of a particular, but rather the depiction of an idealized masculine or feminine form.

The nude was born in ancient Greece, and it combined two Greek convictions. The first Clark calls "the middle form." It is the idea that "the ideal is composed of the average and the habitual." The classic nude does not attempt to display the unique or grotesque, but rather the form common to all men and all women. This "middle way" produces

> the diffused memory of that peculiar physical type developed in Greece between the years 480 and 440 B.C., which in varying degrees of intensity and consciousness furnished the mind of Western man with a pattern of perfection from the Renaissance until the present century.[17]

The second conviction was that of mathematical harmony. The same mindset that drove Pythagoras to discover his theorem gave rise to the idea of proportionality in the human form. "One of the few canons of proportion of which we can be certain is that which, in a female nude, took the same measurement for the distance between the breasts, the distance from the lower breast to the navel, and again from the navel to the division of the legs."[18] To object that no existent woman fits these measurements misses the point; the sculpture il-

---

16 Kenneth Clark, *The Nude: A Study in Ideal Form*, 7.

17 Clark, *The Nude: A Study in Ideal Form*, 14.

18 Clark, *The Nude: A Study in Ideal Form*, 166.

lustrates the mathematical rationality of the world, and turns the female nude into a problem of skill and analysis.

Clark attributes the prevalence of the nude in ancient Greek art to the feeling that "the spirit and body are one…" This sense "manifests itself in their giving to abstract ideas a sensuous, tangible, and for the most part, human form." This glorification of the human body as an expression of the fusion of body and soul has captivated artists from antiquity through the present. Clark adds that

> […] the nude gains its enduring value from the fact that it reconciles several contrary states. It takes the most sensual and immediately interesting object, the human body, and puts it out of reach of time and desire; it takes the most purely rational concept of which mankind is capable, mathematical order, and makes it a delight to the senses; and it takes the vague fears of the unknown and sweetens them by showing that the gods are like men and may be worshipped for their life-giving beauty rather than their death-dealing powers.[19]

The nude is the site of human contradiction and possibility, of embodied spirit communicating reality and truth as understood by the artistic vision. The human form, from ancient Greece onwards, is the way of communicating certain joys and principles unable to exist in a different mode.

Having established his theory, Clark traces the nude across time. Through the image of Apollo, he explores the development of the male nude in Greek sculpture and into Renaissance art.[20] Across two chapters, he explores two dif-

---

19 Clark, *The Nude: A Study in Ideal Form*, 25.

20 Clark, *The Nude: A Study in Ideal Form*, 30–69.

ferent visions of the female nude: the heavenly Venus,[21] and the earthly Venus.[22] Clark focuses on the "plastic elements" of torso length, breast placement, arms, and weight, with a persistent theme of the female form as desirable. As the goddess of love, Venus is an object of desire, but where that desire is placed, whether in the heavens as an unobtainable object of love or in the fields as a plausible woman, shifts over time. "The swift Gothic movement, by which the Dresden *Venus* seems to be lifted above the material world, is replaced by Renaissance satisfaction in the here and now…"[23] By the eighteenth century, *Venus Naturalis* develops into "a definite ideal of feminine beauty, with an unnatural length of limb, an impossible slenderness of body, and a self-conscious elegance of bearing."[24] In contrast to this "definite ideal," Clark showers praise on "the nudes of Rubens." He writes,

> The golden hair and swelling bosoms of his *Graces* are hymns of thanksgiving for abundance, and they are placed before us with the same unself-conscious piety as the sheaves of corn and piled-up pumpkins that decorate a church at harvest festival. […] They are a part of nature; and they embody a view of nature more optimistic than that of the Greeks, for thunder and the treacherous sea, the capricious cruelty of Olympus, are absent.[25]

Clark contends that Rubens' training places him squarely in the tradition of the Greeks and their idealized form. Rubens'

---

21 Clark, *The Nude: A Study in Ideal Form*, 70–117.

22 Clark, *The Nude: A Study in Ideal Form*, 118–172.

23 Clark, *The Nude: A Study in Ideal Form*, 116.

24 Clark, *The Nude: A Study in Ideal Form*, 135.

25 Clark, *The Nude: A Study in Ideal Form*, 140.

procedure was that which has become the dogma of academics: he drew from the antique and copied from his predecessors till certain ideals of completeness were absolutely fixed in his mind; then when he drew from nature he instinctively subordinated the observed facts to the patterns established in his imagination.[26]

Modern artists faced a different dilemma: "how to give the female body that character of wholeness and order which was the discovery of the Greeks and combine such order with a feeling for its warm reality."[27] Renoir exemplifies this quest, and, for Renoir, an answer lay in abandoning the classical mathematical approach in favor of increased realism. *La Baigneuse Blonde* is a success in that the warm vitality of Renoir's wife emerges from the painting through the realistic portrayal of her body; without sacrificing realism, Renoir also conveys the wholeness of her form.[28]

Clark concludes that "art is justified, as man is justified, by the faculty of forming ideas; and the nude makes its first appearance in art theory at the very moment when painters began to claim that their art is an intellectual, not a mechanical, activity."[29] The viability of the nude as a means of artistic communication depends upon some level of idealization. "[...] The antique scheme had involved so complete a fusion of the sensual and the geometric as to provide a kind of armor...once this armor had grown unwearable, either the nude became a dead abstraction or the sexual element became

---

26 Clark, *The Nude: A Study in Ideal Form*, 142.

27 Clark, *The Nude: A Study in Ideal Form*, 166.

28 Clark, *The Nude: A Study in Ideal Form*, 167.

29 Clark, *The Nude: A Study in Ideal Form*, 351.

too insistent."[30] Clark closes his work doubting that contemporary artists can embrace the idealization necessary for the nude to remain viable; perhaps this art form is no longer accessible to contemporary artists.

If Clark's analysis represents the traditional view of the nude, then Richard Leppert's scholarship encapsulates a twenty-first-century progressive view.[31] Leppert begins his analysis explaining that he is

> keen to understand some of the ways that paintings of naked human beings function within the conflicting realms of power throughout any social formation, especially those surrounding differences of class, gender, and race. I am interested in the representation of the naked body as a sight—and sometimes as a spectacle—that is, as an object of display and intense interest upon which the viewer obsessively gazes.[32]

The painting as display invites a gaze that concentrates the power of the viewer upon the subject viewed. Leppert argues that, "[...] all meaning [...] results from social practices that are in a constant state of flux and are under challenge by people holding diverse, often conflicting, interests."[33] Leppert's

---

30 Clark, *The Nude: A Study in Ideal Form*, 361.

31 I am using progressive as an intentional contrast to Clark's traditionalism in naming these schools of thought. This methodology follows the rise of feminist criticism. Two other works of modern art criticism exemplify this progressive view. Margaret Walters, *The Nude Male: A New Perspective* (New York: Penguin Books, 1978). Walters brings a Freudian feminist account to the nude male; her approach is paralleled by the authors collected in Susan Rubin Suleiman, ed. *The Female Body in Western Culture: Contemporary Perspectives* (Cambridge, MA: Harvard University Press, 1986).

32 Richard Leppert, *The Nude: The Cultural Rhetoric of the Body in the Art of Western Modernity*, 2–3.

33 Leppert, *The Nude: The Cultural Rhetoric of the Body in the Art of Western Modernity*, 3.

theory advocates studying a work of art with attention to the political conditions of the viewer rather than the intrinsic meaning to be found in the art itself. Rather than Hegel's view of art as the means of perceiving the Idea, the progressive approach argues that "it makes no sense to think about a painting as though it were 'a delivery van, conveying meaning to the customer.' Viewers do not wait for a painting's meaning to arrive prepackaged. Viewers are active participants in determining meaning."[34]

Leppert argues that "every image embodies historically, socially, and culturally specific, competing and contradictory ways of seeing." Analysis focuses not on the work of art but on the way the viewer experiences that art from a specific context. Leppert explains what this approach brings to the traditional canon of western nudes: "it is critical to emphasize that all this [analysis] will be partial, incomplete, impermanent, and for that matter maybe wrong, but not disinterested. What I seek to do is in fact all that can be done."[35] Leppert poses new questions unasked by earlier generations: "What if the viewer, whether male or female, looking at a nude, is not the presumptive straight viewer, but is instead gay, lesbian, or bisexual? And what of the differences marked by ethnicity, race, class standing, and religious belief?"[36] How does the context of the viewer change his interaction with the painting? That is the first area of interest for the progressive theory of art.

A second area of interest involves the overt sexualization of the nude. While Clark maintained a place for the erotic

---

34 Leppert, *The Nude: The Cultural Rhetoric of the Body*, 5.

35 Leppert, *The Nude: The Cultural Rhetoric of the Body*, 7.

36 Leppert, *The Nude: The Cultural Rhetoric of the Body*, 12.

within the nude, his method of analysis avoided direct consideration of the erotic; if a nude were to stir arousal up directly, both Clark and Scruton contend, the work of art has failed to remain at a distance from the viewer. Leppert proposes a different foundation:

> The desire of men to look at women, and vice versa, whether clothed or naked, is after all deeply informed by sexual necessity, an activity fully sanctioned by society under culturally approved circumstances. Herein lies the problem: There is no roadmap for looking at the body of the other. The look may define desires driven by love or hate, desires mutual and reciprocal, or selfish and self-serving. Accordingly, the rhetoric of a given image is defined by more than itself, by more than it was made to look like. It is driven by the functions to which it is put.[37]

The erotic desire, Leppert suggests, lies at the base of the nude. The nude is the site of interested desire and invites that desire. "[...] The *painted* nude represented nakedness as a state specifically *made for concentrated looking.* [...] The nude in art exists *only* to be seen for what it is: naked. It invites not the averted eye, but the stare."[38] As such, where the eye is directed through lines and lighting that center the gaze becomes crucial. What is revealed as opposed to what is hidden, whether or not the figure is aware of the gaze, whether the figure gazes back at the viewer—these are the questions that Leppert asks of nude paintings that raise awareness of race, gender, and class concerns in the art of the nude. In his afterword, Leppert sums up his approach:

---

37 Leppert, *The Nude: The Cultural Rhetoric of the Body*, 15.

38 Leppert, *The Nude: The Cultural Rhetoric of the Body*, 22.

> Paintings of nudes depend for their effects on the erotics of looking at naked bodies, bodies that in normal life situations would not be available for us to see unclothed. [...] Briefly put, the art nude is not simply 'about' aesthetics (the beautiful form of the human body), because the human body throughout history has served as a "battleground of cultural politics."[39]

Leppert's description of Brockhurst's *Adolescence* is typical. This painting depicts a nude young woman sitting on her knees before a mirror.

> Her emergent womanhood is obvious, but also complicated, principally because of her own gaze, directed toward her own breasts. She is a pretty young woman, whose self-looking seeks the confirmation of her body's sexual development. (The model, Katherine Woodward, eventually became the painter's wife.) The painting is far more direct and uncomplicated than Balthus' *Nude before a Mirror*. Indeed, in this case, the mirror comes close to playing the role often assigned in representations of women as Vanity, a trope anchored not least in the accouterments of makeup that lie on the dresser, together with the coffee pot and cup and saucer that resonate with adulthood. The vanity mirror is tilted so that it provides a full view to her, and to us, of her nakedness. Voyeurism plays a role, and this despite the young woman's self-absorption. Her face is clearly that of a woman at once curious and confident. And though the pose she assumes is entirely natural and typical given the situation and setting, her legs are apart to a degree seldom granted in the art nude. Only the putative privacy of the scene grants the license—or excuse—for such a pose. Finally, her face is clearly that of a woman confident in her

---

39 Leppert, *The Nude: The Cultural Rhetoric of the Body*, 239.

sexual allure, as much a matter of her face, the eyes and eyebrows especially, as of the rest of her body. Her visage suggests thoughtfulness; her facial look articulates an adult sexuality that is less natural, perhaps, and more learned.[40]

This passage illustrates the strength and weakness of Leppert's approach to reading a painting. His explanation of concrete details (her gaze, the coffee pot, the makeup) provides evidence supporting his interpretation, but those concrete details are followed by interpretive leaps about the developing sexuality of the subject. Terms such as *complicated, confirmation,* and *clearly* contribute to constructing a narrative of this painting that shows the progressive theory's assumption of overt sexuality. Leppert sees in this painting a mature, adult sexuality that has been learned; he sees in a teenage girl elements not obvious to another viewer and that do not justify the narrative he builds. This kind of analysis is representative of Leppert's approach.

Clark and Leppert's divergent theories of the nude illustrate the difficulty of interpretation in the twenty-first century. Clark's traditional theory reads the nude as an art form presented by an artist with an idea to communicate; the task is to receive the work of art, and in that reception seek to comprehend the idea that, as Heidegger might have put it, presents itself before the viewer. Leppert's theory, termed "progressive" to contrast it with the traditional theory, rejects the certainty of Clark's formalism and places meaning in the interaction between the viewer and the work of art. This progressive theory prioritizes sexualization, reading the nude as a site for the viewer to experience sexual power dynamics. Of these two views, the first leads to an objective study of the

---

40 Leppert, *The Nude: The Cultural Rhetoric of the Body,* 56.

work of art through which universal meaning can be found. Neither view, however, is fully satisfactory in answering the question of the nude's continued viability as an art form.

Clarke's formalism provides the beginnings of an answer, but by his conclusion he suggests the nude is no longer a viable form in a modernity which rejects the idealized form. Why then does the nude remain as an art form? The answer lies in the way expressing art through human forms allows the artist to tap into universal human experiences through complementary forms.

III. The Dance of Complementarity: An Answer to the Question of the Nude

In 'The Relevance of the Beautiful,' Hans Georg Gadamer builds the aesthetic ideas he developed in *Truth and Method* into a full theory of both art and beauty.[41] Gadamer accepts the role of the viewer in contributing to the formation of meaning, yet limits meaning to the work of art itself. While his theory does much more than comment on the artistic nude, Gadamer provides a foundation for understanding the nude as a universal element of artistic vocabulary. Describing 'the great history of Western art,' Gadamer writes that

> a common language for the common content of our self-understanding has been developed through the Christian art of the Middle Ages and the humanistic revival of Greek and Roman art and literature, right up to the close

---

41 Hans-Georg Gadamer, "The Relevance of the Beautiful: Art as Play, Symbol, and Festival" in *The Relevance of the Beautiful and Other Essays*, trans. Nicholas Walker, ed. Robert Bernasconi (Cambridge, UK: Cambridge University Press, 1996): 3–53.

of the eighteenth century and the great social transformations and political and religious changes with which the nineteenth century began.[42]

This "common language" becomes the foundation for seeing art as a unified field—the artist must understand what has gone before to communicate a fresh vision. The nude sits within this common tradition and resonates with the viewer who shares either the masculine or feminine form idealized in the work of art. The viewer is thus predisposed to understand the visual vocabulary of the nude through participation in one of the sexes, even if the viewer has no knowledge of the historical tradition of the artistic nude. The nude functions as a symbol universally communicable to human viewers. The interplay between male and female forms allows the artist to move freely between different elements of what it means to be human; through contemplation of such works of art, the viewer reaches Gadamer's definition of philosophy: "It is the task of philosophy to discover what is common even in what is different."[43]

Through the visual display of physiological differences between men and women, the viewer is able to recognize the sexes as unique in themselves, yet united in a common humanity. The nude, then, "points toward the sphere of common use and common understanding as the realm of intelligible communication."[44] There is a meaning in the nude which the viewer can comprehend through experiencing the work of art: "...in any encounter with art, it is not the particu-

---

42 Gadamer, *The Relevance of the Beautiful and Other Essays*, 4.

43 Gadamer, *The Relevance of the Beautiful and Other Essays*, 12.

44 Gadamer, *The Relevance of the Beautiful and Other Essays*, 13.

lar but rather the totality of the experienceable world, man's ontological place in it, and above all his finitude before that which transcends him, that is brought to experience."[45] This principle applies specifically to the nude in that through the idealized masculine or feminine form (or both), the viewer is brought to consider all that it means to be male and female in the created order. Such a work of art, Gadamer argues, "signifies an increase in being."[46] By revealing and unfolding that which is present, the work of art makes an increase in being evident to the viewer and summons the viewer to participate in the unfolding of meaning in the world. That meaning, for Gadamer, is not located in Hegel's or Plato's world of ideas, but within the symbol itself:

> Great art shakes us because we are always unprepared and defenseless when exposed to the overarching power of a compelling work. Thus the essence of the symbolic lies precisely in the fact that it is not related to an ultimate meaning that could be recuperated in intellectual terms. The symbol preserves its meaning within itself.[47]

Masculine and feminine forms as symbols give the artist access to different elements of the human experience: the physiological processes of puberty, maturation, and aging; binary elements such as strength/weakness, outward/inward orientation, vertical/horizontal, rough/smooth, dominance/submission. The formalist insights of Clarke and the progressive insights of Leppert are written into the body. The nude becomes a plastic symbol the artist can employ to craft a mean-

---

45 Gadamer, *The Relevance of the Beautiful and Other Essays*, 33.

46 Gadamer, *The Relevance of the Beautiful and Other Essays*, 35.

47 Gadamer, *The Relevance of the Beautiful and Other Essays*, 37.

ing that emerges through the interaction with the audience; rather than being fixed, the nude allows for a developing series of meanings that remain universally accessible because all humans share one of the two sexes. Gadamer has a caution for the intrepid art interpreter: "On the contrary, what the work has to say can only be found within itself."[48] Learning to read a work of art, to appreciate what it says within itself, is the heart of Gadamer's approach. Rather than imputing meaning from an external context, Gadamer, like his master Aristotle before him, insists that whatever meaning is to be found must lie *within* the work itself:

> [...] In the experience of art, we must learn how to dwell upon the work in a specific way. When we dwell upon the work, there is no tedium involved, for the longer we allow ourselves, the more it displays its manifold riches to us. The essence of our temporal experience of art is in learning how to tarry in this way.[49]

Understanding a work of art requires sitting before it and receiving it. In that reception, the viewer participates in the unfolding of meaning within the work of art. In the case of the nude, reception is enabled because the human viewer participates in the masculine or feminine form. This analogical connection enables the universality of the nude as a communicable art form. Gadamer's understanding of art resonates with the foundations of Christian philosophical anthropology. Genesis contains the quintessential statement of human origins: "Then God said, 'Let Us make man in Our image, according to Our likeness' [...] So God created man in His

---

48 Gadamer, *The Relevance of the Beautiful and Other Essays*, 37–38.

49 Gadamer, *The Relevance of the Beautiful and Other Essays*, 45.

own image; in the image of God He created him; male and female he created them" (1:26–27, NKJV). Humans, this passage explains, were created in the literal "likeness" of God, in that they were designed to remind each other of their creator. Their physical form is part of that likeness, and is itself part of human dignity. Genesis represents this dignity through Adam and Eve existing "naked and not ashamed" prior to the Fall. This argument for the dignity of human form gains increasing validity through the doctrine of the incarnation—in the incarnation, the "immortal invisible God" becomes fully corporeal; through the humility of taking on flesh, Christ dignifies the body by elevating it to the divine. The final eschatological vision in Revelation symbolizes this glory of the body by describing resurrected bodies without clothes—the "naked and not ashamed" principle returns in a world without sin, shame, or suffering. Christian theology allows one to view the nude as a promise of that eschatological day when heaven and earth are renewed and the necessity for clothing the body is gone.

The approach to the nude outlined above gives classical educators a way to first recognize the significance of the nude as an art form, and secondly teach students how to approach classic pieces of art, like Botticelli's *Spring*, Michelangelo's *David*, or Rodin's *Thinker*, as rhetorical artifacts. By considering the nude as an artistic choice that communicates, classical educators showcase the divergent views of reality contained in artistic representation. Consider the contrast between Botticelli's *Birth of Venus* and Picasso's *Standing Female Nude*. Botticelli combines classical training with a humanist vision to paint a realistic female form situated within a meaningful cosmos. Analysis of proportion, choice of symbol, mythological figures—all of these and more are perceivable for the classically trained student, and enhance the perception of a meaningful universe that invites exploration and discovery. In contrast, Picasso's nude is a marvel of technical precision and mathematical placement, but the discernment of meaning becomes highly subjective. Instead of a bold declaration of femininity, Picasso's shading hides and obscures; his arrangement of lines suggests rather than states. Here the classical educator can point directly to the core problems of modernity: a loss of certainty, rampant disenchantment, and the replacement of meaning by individual doubt and subjectivity. The nude has a place in upper level humanities courses, and in learning to apprehend the message artists communicate the classical student becomes more attuned to his humanity and to reality itself.

There should be no fear of the nude, and no confusion with pornography. Instead, students need wise teachers who help them see what is good, true, and beautiful in this tradition. In so doing, classical education equips students to step into a world that has lost the ability to understand what it means to be human and celebrate the goodness of God's creation. Tolkien put it best in "Mythopoeia:" "Though now long estranged, / man is not wholly lost nor wholly changed. / Dis-graced he may be, yet is not dethroned, / and keeps the rags of lordship one he owned, / his world-dominion by creative act, / not his to worship the great Artefact." The artistic nude is a human artifact, and as such has a place in education that summons the mind to consider the higher things. In this case, humans access the higher truths of human nature through the visible truths of the human forms. In so doing, humanity celebrates that "male and female he created them."

The Question of the Nude

Joshua Herring is Dean of Classical Education for Thales Academy Apex JH/HS, a PhD student at Faulkner University (Humanities, Literature concentration), and the host for The Optimistic Curmudgeon podcast. He tweets @theOptimisticC3. He and his wife Jennifer live in Wendell, NC.

Wonder and Monsters

by James C. McGlothlin, PhD

Most teachers genuinely hope that the education they provide their students is more than simply the dissemination of information. But for classical educators, this is more than hope. It is a clearly understood goal. As one author recently wrote, the goal of classical education seeks to "educate whole persons through the accumulated wisdom of the ages for a lifetime of flourishing."[1] Classical teachers understand educating "whole persons" as including the formation of good character, seeking to form virtuous traits within students. And wonder, I would argue, is one of these traits. I believe that classical educators desire to see their students filled with wonder and to fall in love with the things of classical education. But what kind of wonder exactly is this?

In referencing J. R. R. Tolkien's secondary world of Middle-earth, theologian Lisa Coutras sees the concept of "wonder" as a "moving encounter with transcendental beauty."[2] I think many would agree that a genuine aesthetic experience

---

[1] Brian A. Williams, "Introducing Principia and Classical Education," *Principia: A Journal of Classical Education* 1, no. 1 (2022): 2.

[2] Lisa Coutras, *Tolkien's Theology of Beauty: Majesty, Splendor, and Transcendence in Middle-earth* (London: Palgrave Macmillan, 2016), 80.

of beauty is one that can indeed instill wonder, especially those taken with the literary works of Tolkien. But can aesthetic experiences with the not-so-beautiful induce wonder as well? And moreover, can aesthetic experiences be utilized, pedagogically and otherwise, in classical education to instill wonder? I believe so.

In the following essay, I will first seek to define the concept of "wonder" that I think educators in general hope for, which I think clarifies why classical educators should seek to evoke a specific kind of wonder within their students. I will then briefly probe how aesthetic experiences can be a source of such wonder, usually connected to beauty. But I will then go on to argue that at least one type of aesthetic experience of ugliness, i.e., good literature that contains monsters, can serve as an avenue for producing this wonder as well. I will defend this claim by appealing to J. R. R. Tolkien's famous literary defense of the monsters within *Beowulf*. I believe that Tolkien's argument generalizes to show that many literary monsters—and thus some aesthetic experiences of ugliness—can be a source of wonder. Since many of the great books used within typical classical education curricula include such entities, I conclude that these aesthetic experiences of ugliness and monstrosity can be conducive to classical education's goal to instill wonder within students.

Wonder and Aesthetic Experience

What exactly is *wonder*? In a recent article,[3] philosophers of education Lynne Wolbert and Anders Schinkel seek to clarify what wonder is and then argue for why it should be considered important within education. They define wonder "as a mode of consciousness in which we experience what we perceive or are contemplating as strange, beyond our powers of comprehension, yet worthy of our attention for its own sake."[4] But why should this mode of consciousness or feeling be considered important within education? To begin making a case for this, Wolbert and Schinkel note that scholars often make a distinction between *wonder at* versus *wonder about*, which they also characterize as the distinction between passive versus active wonder, or contemplative wonder versus inquisitive wonder. They clarify that "whereas *wonder at* is the type of wonder we are 'struck' by and that leaves us lost for words, *wonder about* is inquisitive, explanation-seeking, and in that sense closer to curiosity, though still distinct from it."[5] Wolbert and Schinkel note that *wonder about* "seems 'naturally allied' to education, in the sense that it denotes an eagerness to inquire, a desire to understand, and also…a willingness to suspend judgment."[6] I think most any educator would readily agree that it is good to instill within their students a general

---

[3] Lynne Wolbert and Anders Schinkel, "What Should Schools Do to Promote Wonder?" *Oxford Review of Education* 47, no. 4 (2021): 439–454.

[4] Wolbert and Schinkel, "What Should Schools Do to Promote Wonder?", 440. This is actually a quotation from a 2018 work of Schinkel alone.

[5] Wolbert and Schinkel, "What Should Schools Do to Promote Wonder?", 441. [Italics mine.]

[6] Wolbert and Schinkel, "What Should Schools Do to Promote Wonder?", 443.

inquisitiveness or desire to understand the truth of things, i.e., a *wondering about*-ness. But Wolbert and Schinkel additionally argue that there is also a native connection between education and *wonder at*, i.e., the "struck by" or contemplative type of wonder. What do they see as this educational connection?

Wolbert and Schinkel elucidate that contemplative wonder, or *wondering at*, "is capable of bringing us to the limits of our (present) knowledge or understanding," which they argue can often produce the virtue of intellectual humility within students.[7] For truly *wondering at* "corresponds to the realization of not-knowing, of not really (as in completely) understanding why the world is the way it is, and therefore responding from an appropriate stance of intellectual humility (as opposed to hubris)."[8] Surely this seems like something that teachers would also like to see in their students: being open to the idea that there might be "more than meets the eye." But even more importantly, Wolbert and Schinkel believe that by seeking to instill contemplative wonder within students, teachers not only encourage a sense of humility, but they also believe a sense of mystery can be triggered, an openness and excitement that the world holds more to discover.[9]

As Wolbert and Schinkel have described it, I think classical educators would also largely agree with the goal of seeking to instill the disposition of contemplative wonder within their students. For intellectual humility, and especially a sense of mystery, seem like the sorts of virtuous character traits that classical education hopes to see developed within their

---

[7] Wolbert and Schinkel, "What Should Schools Do to Promote Wonder?", 443–444.

[8] Wolbert and Schinkel, "What Should Schools Do to Promote Wonder?", 444.

[9] Wolbert and Schinkel, "What Should Schools Do to Promote Wonder?", 445.

students. But how exactly can classical teachers do this? Put more concretely, what sort of classical pedagogies, curricula, or class ethos might encourage or instill *wondering at* within students?

I think there are many and various ways to answer that previous question. But one way that I will argue for here is by exploring contemplative wonder's relation to aesthetic experience. Historically, aesthetic experience has usually been associated with human encounters with art and beauty. The late aesthetic philosopher Wladyslaw Tatarkiewicz noted that the traditional "notion of beauty [usually] extended only to that which evokes aesthetic experience."[10] And though beauty was for centuries in the West often considered the primary focus of aesthetic experience, this perspective has been in decline for quite some time now. For at least a century or more, beauty has not been seen even as a primary goal of the arts.[11] In fact, from the layman's perspective, contemporary art might sometimes seem more taken with ugliness than anything else.

Nevertheless, aesthetic pleasure, which is often accompanied by an experience of wonder, is still something that most any person can attest to experiencing. Whether we prefer Bach or Beyoncé, *Citizen Kane* or *Titanic*, a lush landscape or a desert scene, we are all familiar with having been deeply moved by some sort of aesthetic experience. But whereas many experiences of beauty may be an obvious source of wonder, can the same be said of at least some experiences of

---

10 Wladyslaw Tatarkiewicz, "The Great Theory of Beauty and Its Decline," *The Journal of Aesthetics and Art Criticism* 31, no. 2 (1972), 166. He also notes that beauty was also understood more broadly as including moral beauty. For simplicity here, I am laying that further complication aside.

11 Crispin Sartwell, "Beauty," in *The Stanford Encyclopedia of Philosophy*, ed. Edward Zalta, (March 5, 2023). https://plato.stanford.edu/archives/sum2022/entries/beauty/.

the less-than-beautiful as well? I believe so. Note the following comparative list of typical synonyms for *beautiful* and *ugly*, compiled by the late novelist and philosopher Umberto Eco:

> If we examine the synonyms of *beautiful* and *ugly*, we see that while what is considered *beautiful* is: pretty, cute, pleasing, attractive, agreeable, lovely, delightful, fascinating, harmonious, marvellous, delicate, graceful, enchanting, magnificent, stupendous, sublime, exceptional, fabulous, wonderful, fantastic, magical admirable, exquisite, spectacular, splendid, and superb; what is *ugly* is: repellent, horrible, horrendous, disgusting, disagreeable, grotesque, abominable, repulsive, odious, indecent, foul, dirty, obscene, repugnant, frightening, abject, monstrous, horrid, horrifying, unpleasant, terrible, terrifying, frightful, nightmarish, revolting, sickening, fetid, fearsome, ignoble, ungainly, displeasing, tiresome, offensive, deformed, and disfigured (not to mention how horror an also manifest itself in areas traditionally assigned to the beautiful, such as the fabulous, the fantastic, the magical and the sublime).
>
> The sensibility of the common speaker reveals that, whereas all the synonyms for *beautiful* could be conceived as a reaction of disinterested appreciation, almost all of the synonyms for *ugly* contain a reaction of disgust, if not of violent repulsion, horror, or fear.[12]

Bracketing Eco's claim that the synonyms for *beautiful* could all be conceived as "disinterested appreciation," Eco helpfully summarizes that *ugliness* tends to "contain a reaction of disgust." And even if Eco has overstated his point here, there does indeed seem to be something about our typical adjectives and descriptors of *ugliness* that tends to suggest more redolent

---

[12] Umberto Eco, ed. *On Ugliness*, trans. Alastair McEwen (New York: Rizzoli, 2011), 16.

or visceral-type experiences than our customary adjectives for *beauty*. This observation, I think, is suggestive. It seems to me that the seemingly more evocative nature of the non-beautiful suggests that at least some aesthetic experiences of ugliness could operate as pedagogical means to help instill contemplative wonder within their students, as described above. That might sound far-fetched. But for the remainder of this essay, I will provide reasons that seek to support at least one instance of this claim, appealing to an argument from the late philologist and renowned fantasy writer J. R. R. Tolkien.

Tolkien on the Importance of Monsters

In 1936 J. R. R. Tolkien gave the annual Sir Israel Gollancz Memorial Lecture to the British Academy. This talk was later published as "Beowulf: The Monsters and the Critics." The primary point of this lecture and later essay was the offering of a defense for studying the Anglo-Saxon poem *Beowulf* as, primarily, a poetic work. That proposition may sound tautologous; but Tolkien was convinced that it needed to be emphasized because the way *Beowulf* had been largely studied in his day seemed to forget or obscure this seemingly obvious point. Tolkien memorably characterizes the situation in the "whole industry" of *Beowulf* criticism with the following allegory:

> A man inherited a field in which was an accumulation of old stone, part of an older hall. Of the old stone some had already been used in building the house in which he actually lived, not far from the old house of his fathers. Of the rest he took some and built a tower. But his friends perceived at once (without troubling to climb the steps)

that these stones had formerly belonged to a more ancient building. So they pushed the tower over, with no little labour, in order to look for hidden carvings and inscriptions, or to discover whence the man's distant forefathers had obtained their building material. Some suspecting a deposit of coal under the soil began to dig for it, and forgot even the stones. They all said: 'This tower is most interesting.' And even the man's own descendants, who might have been expected to consider what he had been about, were heard to murmur: 'He is such an odd fellow! Imagine his using these old stones just to build a nonsensical tower! Why did not he restore the old house? He had no sense of proportion.' But from the top of that tower the man had been able to look out upon the sea (7–8).[13]

This allegorical depiction captures Tolkien's frustration that scholarly critics could seemingly neither analyze nor enjoy the tower (i.e., the poem *Beowulf*) simply as a tower (i.e., as a poem). Rather, from Tolkien's perspective, their scholarly endeavors had allegorically "pushed the tower over." And in doing so, as Tolkien's metaphor seeks to make plain, they were thus unable to appreciate what the original *Beowulf* poet had appreciated and still invites all readers to enjoy, to "look out upon the sea," the ability to appreciate a vista or viewpoint that can only be seen when reading the story of *Beowulf* as the original poet had intended, i.e., as a poem and epic.

One of the things that I find most interesting in Tolkien's defense of studying *Beowulf* as a poem, is that he ends up spending most of his time in this essay defending the poet's use of monsters (i.e., ugly entities). Evidently, most scholars

---

13 All parenthetic page references in this essay are to J. R. R. Tolkien, "Beowulf: The Monsters and the Critics" in *The Monsters and the Critics and Other Essays*, ed. Christopher Tolkien (London: HarperCollins Publishers, 2006). Within these quotations I have kept the original British spellings of words.

in the early twentieth century considered this facet of *Beowulf* as somewhat embarrassing, and quite at odds with the literary merit of the work. In stark contrast, Tolkien saw the monsters as both necessary and important to the theme of *Beowulf*. Let us now look at his argument in some detail.

"Beowulf: The Monsters and the Critics" is today recognized as a significant piece of *Beowulf* scholarship. As Verlyn Flieger notes, it "stands as the most important and influential piece of work on that poem in the twentieth century."[14] But in 1936, Tolkien's talk and later essay was going very much against the scholarly grain. At that time, most *Beowulf* critics saw the poem as a "puzzling and seriously flawed work," including what they saw as the unfortunate focus upon monstrous entities.[15] But Tolkien saw the appearance of monsters within *Beowulf* much differently and defended the poet's use of them; for Tolkien understood that monstrous entities could embody important themes and do so in very powerful and wonder-inspiring ways. Thus, Tolkien's essay is more than simply a defense of the monstrous entities within *Beowulf*, it also operates as a defense of monsters within good literature more generally.

Tolkien summarizes that many critics in his day believed that *Beowulf*'s "weakness lies in placing the unimportant things at the centre and the important on the outside" (5). These scholars thought it was perhaps understandable that ancient and medieval simpletons would include monsters within their stories; but what a literary mistake to make them so central to their stories! As Tolkien's contemporaries saw it, the poetic

---

14 Verlyn Flieger, *Splintered Light: Logos and Language in Tolkien's World*, rev. ed. (Kent, OH: Kent State University Press, 2002), 13.

15 Flieger, *Splintered Light*, 13.

talent of *Beowulf* had "all been squandered on an unprofitable theme: as if Milton had recounted the story of Jack and the Beanstalk in noble verse" (13). For these scholars seemingly just could not "admit that the monsters are anything but a sad mistake" (16).

But Tolkien, as a lover of the poem as well as a scholar, strongly disagreed for he understood how the monsters of *Beowulf* intricately served the theme of the poem. And what exactly did Tolkien understand its theme to be? Within the essay Tolkien begins a bit sheepishly about stating it outright, for he notes that "the significance of a myth is not easily to be pinned on paper by analytical reasoning. It is at its best when it is presented by a poet who feels rather than makes explicit what his theme portends" (15). This is well put since poetic and literary expression has long been recognized as capable of expressing truth in a way that more straightforward propositional expression simply cannot. Theologian and poet Malcolm Guite makes this point succinctly in noting that the human faculty of imagination, which is what engages with poetry, "'apprehends' more than cool reason ever 'comprehends'."[16] Thus, when someone attempts to explain the content of poetic or literary form, one either is unable to do so or seriously risks damaging the content of what was originally communicated. Tolkien recognized this in explaining the theme of *Beowulf*: "Its defender is thus at a disadvantage: unless he is careful, and speaks in parables, he will kill what he is studying by vivisection, and he will be left with a formal or mechanical allegory, and, what is more, probably with one that will not work" (15).

---

16   Malcolm Guite, *Lifting the Veil: Imagination and the Kingdom of God* (Baltimore, MD: Square Halo Books, 2021), 21. Guite credits Shakespeare for this terminological distinction.

Nevertheless, Tolkien goes on to argue that the *Beowulf* poet had devoted his work primarily to the theme of the inevitability of Beowulf's final defeat and death, drawing "the struggle in different proportions, so that we may see man at war with the hostile world, and his inevitable overthrow in Time" (18). As anyone who has read the poem knows, there are several explicit Christian references throughout *Beowulf*. But the pessimistic and pagan Norse idea of fate, or the *wyrd*, is clearly in the foreground. As a scholar of ancient Germanic languages, Tolkien believed that *Beowulf* was not simply a syncretistic stew of Christian and pagan elements, nor a "confusion, a half-hearted or a muddled business, but a fusion that has occurred *at a given point* of contact between old and new, a product of thought, and deep emotion" (20). The poet of *Beowulf*, who was more than likely a monk, knew the older days and traditions of his Norse context. And "one thing he knew clearly: those days were heathen—heathen, noble, and hopeless" (22). And Tolkien recognized the poet as making use of these readily available themes. In the old pagan view, "the monsters had been the foes of the gods...and [believed that] within Time the monsters would win" (22). Furthermore, Tolkien noted, the poet knew that "a Christian was (and is) still like his forefathers a mortal hemmed in a hostile world. The monsters remained the enemies of mankind, the infantry of the old war, and became inevitably the enemies of the one God,...the eternal Captain of the new" (22). Tolkien spends some significant space in his essay making the case for this point, claiming the author of *Beowulf*, despite his central use of fictional monsters and pagan ideas, was

> still concerned primarily with *man on earth*, rehandling in a new perspective an ancient theme: that man, each man

and all men, all their works shall die. A theme no Christian need despise. Yet this theme plainly would not be so treated, but for the nearness of a pagan time. The shadow of its despair, if only as a mood, as an intense emotion of regret, is still there. The worth of defeated valour in this world is deeply felt. As the poet looks back into the past, surveying the history of kings and warriors in the old traditions, he sees that all glory (or as we might say 'culture' or 'civilization') ends in night. The solution of that tragedy is not treated—it does not arise out of the material. We get in fact a poem from a pregnant moment of poise, looking back into the pit, by a man learned in old tales who was struggling, as it were, to get a general view of them all, perceiving their common tragedy of inevitable ruin, and yet feeling this more *poetically* because he was himself removed from the direct pressure of its despair. He could from without, but still feel immediately and from within, the old dogma: despair of the event, combined with faith in the value of doomed resistance. He was dealing with the great temporal tragedy, and not yet writing an allegorical homily in verse (23).

This is also why Tolkien argues earlier in the essay that it is a mistake to understand *Beowulf* as "the hero of an heroic lay." Rather, more simply and more straightforwardly, the poet presents Beowulf not as a hero but as simply *"a man, and that for him and many is sufficient tragedy"* (18, italics original). Tolkien surmised that beneath what we recognize today as typical motifs of the horror genre lay a truer horror and a truer tragedy, which the Christian poet was attempting to communicate within this pagan fictional world: the world of men—*this* world—is hostile to his happiness and existence, and man is ultimately destined to die. And as Tolkien said above, this is "a theme no Christian need despise" (23). The Christian poet of *Beowulf* understood that Beowulf's iron shield that he bore against the monsters of the poem, "was not yet the breastplate of righteousness, nor the shield of faith for the quenching of all the fiery darts of the wicked" (23).[17]

Summarizing then, Tolkien understood the theme of *Beowulf* to be about not only the particular and inevitable death of a warrior in his fictional world, but the general and inevitable death of all mankind in our world. For us, the poem of *Beowulf* is ancient, "and yet," notes Tolkien, "its maker was telling of things already old and weighted with regret, and he expended his art in making keen that touch upon the heart which sorrows that are both poignant and remote" (33). Thus, "it is not an irritating accident that the tone of the poem is so high and its theme so low. It is the theme in its deadly seriousness that begets the dignity of tone" (18–19). And what better way to communicate that tragic theme in this milieu? This was Tolkien's main point in the essay: "the monsters are not an inexplicable blunder of taste; they are essential, fundamentally allied to the underlying ideas of the poem, which give it its lofty tone and high seriousness" (19). In other words, it is not just the theme of death alone that gives *Beowulf* its powerful effect, but death by monsters.[18] Tolkien concludes the essay with this summary thought: "It is just because the main foes in *Beowulf* are inhuman that the story is larger and more significant than [other] imaginary poem[s] of a great king's fall. It glimpses the cosmic and moves with the thought of all men concerning the fate of human life and efforts; it stands amid but above the

---

17 Tolkien is alluding to the spiritual armor metaphor of the apostle Paul in Ephesians 5:13–17.

18 I am indebted to Verlyn Flieger for this insightful point: Flieger, *Splintered Light*, 17.

petty wars of princes, and surpasses the dates and limits of historical periods, however important" (33).

Conclusion

I am utterly convinced by Tolkien's essay. *Beowulf* should be read first and foremost as a poem, and as an epic. Rather than dismantling the tower to analyze its components, Tolkien was suggesting we travel up to the top of the tower as the original tower builder, the original poet, meant us to. What vistas do we see from there? What was the *Beowulf* poet attempting to communicate? Tolkien convincingly argues that the monstrous beings of *Beowulf* were essential components for communicating the stark theme of the poem. The profundity of the tragic message of *Beowulf*, the message of mankind at odds with a dangerous world, is powerfully communicated in its use of the horrific beings of Grendel, his mother, and the great dragon.

Furthermore, I would add that the poet's use of these literary monsters suggests that reality is neither saccharine nor morally neutral. The existence of monsters within the story also denies that death and evil are easily overcome or banal. But note that these claims I have just stated in propositional form do *not* communicate their meaning as effectively as the verse of *Beowulf* does. The story communicates its truth by a sense of wonder. Tolkien helps to remind us that *Beowulf*, when read and seriously enjoyed, encourages contemplative wonder.

Moreover, this is true not only of *Beowulf*. I believe that Tolkien's argument can be aptly applied to most any great work of literature that contains these monstrous elements, such as Homer's *Odyssey*, Dante's *Divine Comedy*, Spenser's *The Faerie Queen*, even Lewis's *The Chronicles of Narnia*. For serious books within classical education that have horrific elements, like monsters, rarely include such simply for decorative flair. Rather, the aesthetic experiences that come through these elements in such works communicates ideas in powerful, wonder-filled ways. And I am sure that many classical teachers have realized and understood this. All that I am highlighting in this essay is that enjoyable and powerful aesthetic experience can include more than beauty *and* that one component of such aesthetic experiences is that of instilling contemplative wonder, bringing us to a realization that there is more to the world than meets the eye.

I am sure that this point can be more easily seen and appreciated when we think about teaching students the magnitude of the universe in astronomy or the utter complexity of DNA in biology. But, as I think Tolkien helps us to see, this can also be realized in the study of great works of literature. Students, and all of us, clearly need to experience the wonder of beauty. But may we also realize that we sometimes need monsters as well.

□

James McGlothlin is Associate Professor of Philosophy and Theology at Bethlehem College in Minneapolis, Minnesota. His research interests include the history and philosophy of ethics and aesthetics. In his free time, he enjoys reading fantasy and horror literature, and when with his wife Cindy, riding bicycles or going on hikes. He is currently working on an aesthetic theodicy project: how to reconcile the existence of darkness, ugliness, and monstrosity in light of the all-powerful, all-beautiful God of Christianity.

kepler

Empowering Families by Liberating Teachers

The Consortium: A Journal of Classical Christian Education is underwritten by Kepler Education.

Kepler, LLC is a marketplace for classical Christian education operated by a consortium of independent classical educators unified by a shared vision for student flourishing.

Learn more at www.kepler.education